DORLING KINDERSLEY DK EYEWITNESS BOOKS

POND
&RIVER

Swan mussel shell

Water snail shell

Common reed

Common reed fruiting head

Otter skull

Kingfisher skull

Mayfly

Reed-mace fruit

Mallard egg

Reed bunting nest and eggs

Great diving beetle

Kingfisher wing

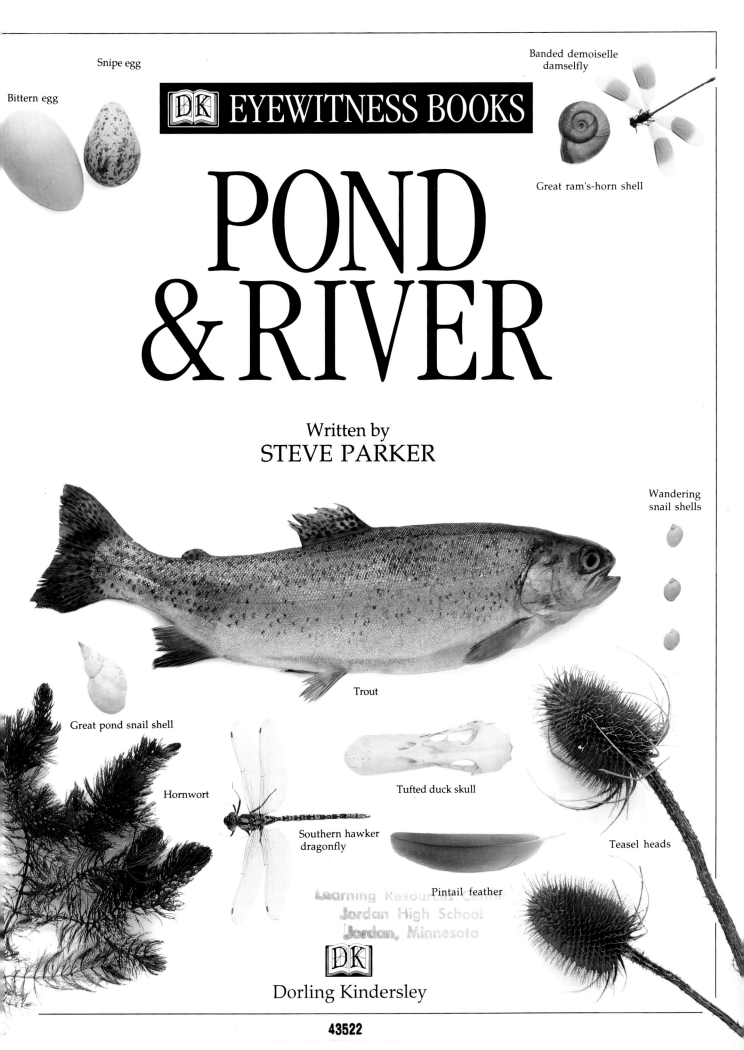

Snipe egg

Bittern egg

Banded demoiselle damselfly

DK EYEWITNESS BOOKS

Great ram's-horn shell

POND & RIVER

Written by
STEVE PARKER

Wandering snail shells

Trout

Great pond snail shell

Hornwort

Tufted duck skull

Southern hawker dragonfly

Teasel heads

Pintail feather

DK
Dorling Kindersley

Curly waterweed

Floating pondweed leaves

River snail

Yellow flag seeds

Water bird feather

Fern

Water beetle

Bog pondweed leaves

![DK logo] **Dorling Kindersley**
LONDON, NEW YORK, AUCKLAND, DELHI, JOHANNESBURG,
MUNICH, PARIS and SYDNEY

For a full catalog, visit
DK www.dk.com

Water starwort

Azolla water fern

Water boatman

Three-spined sticklebacks

Dragonfly larva

Water bird feather

Project editor Sophie Mitchell
Art editor Pamela Harrington
Managing art editor Jane Owen
Special photography Philip Dowell
Editorial consultants
The Staff of the Natural History Museum, London

This Eyewitness ® Book has been conceived by
Dorling Kindersley Limited and Editions Gallimard

© 1988 Dorling Kindersley Limited
This edition © 2000 Dorling Kindersley Limited
First American Edition, 1988

Published in the United States by
Dorling Kindersley Publishing, Inc.
95 Madison Avenue
New York NY 10016
4 6 8 10 9 7 5 3

Dorling Kindersley books are available at special discounts for bulk
purchases for sales promotions or premiums. Special editions, including
personalized covers, excerpts of existing guides, and corporate imprints
can be created in large quantities for specific needs. For more information,
contact Special Markets Dept., Dorling Kindersley Publishing, Inc.,
95 Madison Ave., New York, NY 10016; Fax: (800) 600-9098

Water lily leaves

Library of Congress Cataloging-in-Publication Data
Parker, Steve.
Pond & river/written by Steve Parker; photography by Philip Dowell.
p. cm. — (Eyewitness Books)
Includes index.
Summary: A photo essay about the range of plants and animals found in
freshwater throughout the year, examining the living conditions and
survival mechanisms of creatures dwelling at the edge of the water, on its
surface, or under the mud.
I. Pond ecology — Juvenile literature. 2. Stream ecology — Juvenile
literature. I. Dowell, Philip. II. Title. III. Title: Pond and river.
QH541.5.P63P37 2000 574.5'26322 — dc19 88-1575
ISBN 0-7894-5839-X (pb)
ISBN 0-7894-5838-1 (hc)

Color reproduction by Colourscan, Singapore
Printed in China by Toppan Printing Co. (Shenzhen) Ltd.

Mare's-tail

Great pond snails

Hornwort

Contents

Great ram's-horn shell

Fool's watercress leaf

Hornwort leaf

6
Spring plants
8
Spring animals
10
Early summer plants
12
Early summer animals
14
Midsummer plants
16
Midsummer animals
18
The pond in autumn
20
The pond in winter
22
Freshwater fish
26
The trout
28
Waterfowl
30
Water birds
32
Rushes and reeds
34
The reed bed
36
Waterside mammals
38
Frogs, toads, and newts

40
Hunters in the water
42
Floating flowers
44
Plants at the pond's surface
46
Underwater weeds
48
Dragonflies and damselflies
50
Insects in the water
52
Freshwater shells
54
The head of the river
56
Life along the riverbank
58
The river's mouth
60
The saltmarsh
62
Study and conservation
64
Index

Spring plants

A<small>FTER THE DULL, COLD DAYS</small> of winter, spring is here at last. There are more hours of sunlight each day, and temperatures are rising. For plants, it is the beginning of the annual race for a place in the sun. In general, the tiny algae, duckweeds, and other small plants are first to show their growth, since each one is small and needs relatively little food. But around the pond, and in marshy areas elsewhere, the irises, reeds, and other colonizers are also showing new green shoots and leaves. All the plants shown below were collected from around a pond on a spring day. They give an idea of the species you may find, although there will always be variations from pond to pond.

WARNING
All the plants and animals shown in this book were collected only after gaining permission from the organizations in charge. Always observe the wildlife and country codes when collecting specimens.

Water crowfoot is one of the first pond flowers to appear in spring

Great pond sedge

Mature m... flower he...

REEDS REBORN
New shoots of reed grass spring up from a tangle of rooting stems and roots in the marshy area next to the pond or river. One of last year's stems still stands erect, tall as a person.

Immature female flower head

Last year's stem survived the winter

Common sedge

POLLEN AT ITS TIP
One of the male flower heads at the tip of this great pond sedge already has its stamens open and is shedding yellow pollen. The female flower heads are carried lower on the stem; these are not yet mature.

Reed grass

SEDGE AT THE EDGE
Beside the pond grows common sedge, its flower heads not quite fully opened as yet.

SPRING LILAC
Some of the earliest splashes of color around the pond are the pale lilac blooms of the cuckoo flower, or lady's-smock.

New spring growth

Lady's-smock

6

SEASON OF CATKINS
Willow trees, common on lake and river edges, greet spring with a fine display of furry catkins. These are the tree's flowers. Early bees and other insects visit the flowers for nectar and carry off the tree's pollen. The wind also blows pollen from the golden male catkins to the greenish female ones, which are usually borne on a different tree.

Female catkins

Female catkins

Goat (pussy) willow

Weeping willow

Crack willow

FLAGS STILL FURLED
The yellow flag iris will soon be in bloom. Here, the new leaves grow up from the thick, spreading, underground stem. From their swordlike shape this plant has gotten another name, the sword flag.

Yellow flag

Swordlike leaves

THE PUSS MOTH
The caterpillar of this moth feeds on the leaves of poplars and sallows (a kind of willow). Both trees grow in damp or moist soil, so puss moths and their caterpillars are often seen near ponds and rivers.

Male catkins covered in yellow pollen

Last year's stem

KING OF THE FLOWERS
The brilliant yellow flowers of the marsh marigold, or kingcup, decorate pond edges and other damp areas almost as soon as the snows melt away. A snail or some other plant-eater has already made a meal of one new leaf.

WATER PLANTAIN
A pale, woody stem is all that is left of last year's 3 ft (1 m) spray of flowers (p. 57). New leaves grow from a bulblike base. Despite its name, the water plantain is not one of the true plantains, enemy of all lawn gardeners.

New spring growth

Marsh marigold

Leaf damaged by snail

Meadow rue

Delicate, notched leaves

Water plantain

SPRING FLUSH
A young meadow rue bears its first flush of delicately notched leaves. It prefers damp meadows and pond or stream banks.

Spring animals

As THE SPRING SUN'S WARMTH spreads through the water, animals begin to stir themselves from among the weeds and mud at the bottom of the pond. It is a time of urgent new life. Frogs and toads, fish and newts, are courting, mating, and laying eggs. Their offspring soon hatch in the warming water, eager to cash in on the spring burst of life that provides food for all. "Cold-blooded" aquatic creatures become more active with the rising water temperature, and in a mild spring the smaller ponds, which warm up faster than large ones, are soon seething with newborn snails, insects, amphibians, and many other creatures.

Frog spawn

Protective jelly
surrounding e

Black e

*Tiny tadpoles from
a cool pond*

*Tadpoles from
a warm pond*

This engraving of
a water flea shows
its complex anatomy

THE SPAWN IS BOR
As early as January, ad
frogs gather in ponds to mate and spaw
or lay eggs (pp. 38-39). Around March t
female lays up to 3,000 eggs, fertilized by t
male, who clings to her back. The wate
absorbing jelly around each egg swel
and soon the whole mass is mar
times her body siz

BIG BROTHERS AND SISTERS
Tadpoles hatch from spawn some two to
three weeks after laying. The warmer t
water, the faster they develop. Here,
common frog tadpoles from a large, cool
pond, only two weeks out of their eggs,
mingle with four-weekers from a small pon
that warmed up more quickly.

Common toad

Dry, warty skin

BORN ONTO THEIR FOOD
Each adult pond snail lays
up to 400 eggs, buried in
a jelly-like "rope" attached
to the underside of a submerged
leaf on which the young snails will
feed (p. 52).

A NEW LEAF
In spring, water snails
lay their eggs under
leaves like these
water lily
leaves.

Water lily leav

*Protective
jelly*

Snail
eggs

Pond
snails

Water
fleas

SPRING BLOOM
Water fleas and other
tiny animals and plants
bring a pea-soup look to
many ponds in spring. This is the
early "bloom" of microorganisms
that provides food for larger creatures.

TWO SEXES IN ONE
Many adult pond snails
are hermaphrodites,
having both male and female
reproductive organs.

*Damage to leaf edge
caused by natural splitting*

KING OF THE BEETLES
The great diving beetle is the king of the carnivores in many small ponds, feeding on tadpoles, small fish, and almost anything else it can catch. In fact the dull, furrowed "back" (hard wing covers) on this one indicates it is not a king but a queen - a female. The male's wing cases are smooth and shiny.

COND SPRING
is young water beetle, common in all ponds and ditches, may well be ebrating its second birthday. vo years ago it was an egg, in that tumn a larva, last spring a pupa, d last summer a newly erged adult.

FIRST SPRING
A water beetle larva has large jaws ready to tackle and eat any small creature the spring pond has to offer. Some species stay as larvae for two years or more before changing into adults (p. 51).

Female beetles have furrowed wing covers

Pale-green fronds

Water beetle

SOME WEEKS TO TAKEOFF
A mayfly larva displays its characteristic three tails. Despite its name, this larva might become adult and fly off in April or June (p. 50).

Water beetle larva

Erpobdella leech

Mayfly larva

Water slater

Male newt

Crest along male's back

Duckweed

OKING
R A WORM
e erpobdella leech ps through the water search of a meal. This ch does not suck blood, t attacks worms and er soft-bodied small atures and swallows em whole.

FINDING A MATE
The female water slater piggybacks the male as he fertilizes the eggs, which she keeps in a pouch under her body.

BREEDING NEWTS
In spring the male newt develops a crest along his back and black spots over his skin. The female's skin remains olive-brown.

Female newt

GREEN CEILING
In the spring sunshine, duckweed soon spreads across the pond (p. 44). The tiny fronds provide food for snails and insect larvae.

mmon g

Smooth, shiny skin

EARLY FLOWERS
The water crowfoot is an aquatic type of buttercup. The broad, flat leaves that float on the surface shade the water beneath, providing a good hiding place for fish.

E-YEAR-OLDS
addition to eeding adults, awn, and dpoles, you nay also find last year's babies around the pond in spring (pp. 38-41).

Leaves that float on the surface are flat and broad

READY TO MATE
In spring, the male stickleback's throat and underside turn bright red (a red tinge can even be seen from above, as on the male shown here). In this breeding coloration, he entices the female to lay eggs in the nest he has built on the pond bed (p. 25).

Frogs lose their tail soon after emerging

Leaves that grow under water are finely divided

Male stickleback

Female stickleback

Early summer plants

THE RICHNESS AND VARIETY of a pond's animal life depend on plants. Only a good growth of greenery, such as the plants shown here (all collected from a pond in early summer) will provide food, shelter, and nesting sites for aquatic creatures. The kinds and amounts of plant life depend largely on how much sunlight the pond receives. Sunlight is the energy that ultimately powers life - and in summer it is in plentiful supply. Green plants capture the sun's light energy and transform it into chemical energy in their tissues - a process known as photosynthesis. When a herbivore eats a plant, it takes in some of this chemical energy; when a carnivore (animal-eater) eats the herbivore, it gets what the herbivore took from the plant. Along the way, each plant and animal uses up some energy itself, changing it into movement, new body tissues, seeds, or eggs. A pond heavily shaded by trees will soon lose its vitality and richness of plants - and so, of animals.

GROWING TALL
The straight stems of the common reed are already shouldering their way above most other plants (p. 32). Most of the handsome flower heads do not appear until late summer.

STRAPS OF LEAV
The firm, strap-shap leaves of reed mace sta as tall as a person. In a fe weeks most of the famili "brown poker" flowe will be visible (p. 3

RAGGED PETALS
The ragged robin's pink petals have four long straggly lobes. The plant thrives in many damp places, from pond banks to marshes.

Flowers appear for about two months in early summer

Ragged robin

Water arum

Tufted seeds

FLUFFY TUFTS
Cotton grass, an inhabitant of marshes and boggy pond sides, is a member of the sedge family (p. 32). When the ripe fruits develop they have unmistakable tufts of cottony hairs that catch the wind and disperse the seeds within.

UNPLEASANT SCENT
Common figwort is found on pond and stream banks, and also damp shrublands and woods. The central flower bud in each group is the first to open; the unpleasant scent attracts pollinating wasps.

Central flower bud is first to open in early summer

Cotton grass

Common-reed stem

Common figwort

RICHLY ROOTED
Water arum has thick, spreading stems with dense roots.

Roots stabilize plant in shifting pond-edge soil

RIPENING FRUITS
The gray willow's leaves are more rounded than the spear-shaped leaves of the weeping willow. This tree, also called the sallow, is developing fluff-covered fruits from the female catkins (p. 7). Like most willows, it roots well in damp ground by ponds and rivers.

Reed mace

EMERGING FLOWERS
The yellow flowers of the yellow flag iris are just beginning to unfurl from their protective bracts (sheaths).

Female catkin ____

Fluffy fruits

SEDGE SEEDS
In summer the fuzzy yellowish flower heads of false fox sedge (p. 33) darken to ripe seeds ready to be scattered along the pond bank.

Bract

Style *Petal*

Sepal

Gray willow

Darkening seed heads

PETALS AND SEPALS
The "petals" of the yellow flag are, in fact, made up of sepals, petals, and styles (the female parts of the flower that help to receive the pollen).

Cone

False fox sedge

Yellow flag

CONE BEARER
The marsh horsetail grows best in very moist ground and shallow water. Horsetails do not bear flowers; instead they have conelike structures at their stem tips (compare with the mare's-tail on p. 12).

Marsh horsetail

11

Early summer animals

Silver water beetle, wing cases lifted to show wings

EARLY SUMMER is a time of thinning out and fattening up for pond animals. The swarms of young tadpoles, insect larvae, and water snail feed greedily on the abundant plant growth of this season (pp. 10-11). But they are gradually thinned out by larger predatory creatures, such as beetle larvae and dragonfly nymphs (p. 48), newts, and small fish. These grow fat and in their turn may be eaten by larger creatures, from frogs to fish, by visiting birds like herons, and perhaps by water shrew, mink, and other mammals. And so the food chain of the pond builds up: plants first, then herbivores (plant-eaters), to carnivores (meat-eaters). But this is not the end. Death comes to all and, when it does, creatures such as water slaters move in to consume plant and animal remains. Droppings of all creatures enrich the water, providing minerals and other raw materials for fresh plant growth. So the nutrients go around and around, being recycled in the miniature ecosystem that is the pond.

Common toad

Tadpoles with developing back legs

GOOD-BYE FOR THIS YEAR
A few of the dozens of breeding toads may still be hanging around near the pond. But most have now gone to their favorite damp corners, in hedges, under logs, and among the undergrowth They will not return to the pond until next spring.

PETAL-LESS FLOWERS
Mare's-tail is a shallow-w plant of ponds and streams. The numerous tiny pond creatures of this season squirm and swim around its stems. Where the leaves join the stem, it bears tiny flowers without petals.

BACK LEGS FIRST
Frog tadpoles are now fewer in number; many of their siblings have been eaten by fish, newts, diving beetles, and dragonfly nymphs. They have their back legs, which appear after about seven weeks. This change in body shape, from tadpole to adult frog, is called "metamorphosis."

Great pond snail

GROWN UP
This great pond snail is nearing full size, about 2 in (5 cm) long. It slides slowly over the bottom of the pond, eating decaying plant remains.

Mare's-tail

Engraving of water boatman
showing feathery limbs

...ING UP
...s fully grown emperor dragonfly nymph
... terrorized its small pond for two years,
... one of the chief predators. It will soon be
...mbing up a plant stem and out of
... water for its final
...lt (p. 48).

Emperor dragonfly nymph

Mayfly nymph
attacked by
dragonfly
nymph

Water beetle
larvae

Flatworm

Silver water
beetle (p. 51)

ROWING IN WEED
Two water boatmen (p. 51) scull their
way through ivy-leaved duckweed.
Unlike the lesser duckweed (p. 9),
this plant floats just below the
water's surface.

LONG-NECKED LARVA
This flamingo-necked
aquatic larva will
become a diving
beetle, a member
of the same group
as the great diving
beetle (p. 51).

Leeches are often
found under stones
in the water

Water mites inhabit most ponds and streams
and are a few millimeters long

LEAFY SHADE
Frogbit leaves have sprouted from buds that
survived the winter (p. 45), providing shade
for water creatures as the summer sun gains
warmth. The flowers will not develop until
mid to late summer.

Water
crowfoot

CARPET OF FLOWERS
Water crowfoot is by now carpeting
many pond surfaces with its white
petals and mats of surface leaves.
The feathery trailing greenery also
belongs to this plant; it is its
underwater leaves (p. 9).

Frogbit

Carp fry

Carp fry

BABY CARP
These carp fry
(under one year
old)hatched out
several weeks
ago, after their
mother laid
about half a
million eggs.
Carp do not
lay eggs unless
the water is
about 65° F
(18° C) or above.
This time next
year, they may
tip the scales at
2.2 lb (1 kg).

13

Midsummer plants

THE MIDSUMMER POND is fringed with blooms of all colors, from the dusky pink of hemp agrimony to the many yellows of St.-John's-wort and the buttercups, and the tall purple loosestrife and rosy-red great willow herb. Out on the water, lilies of various colors and the bright pink blooms of water bistort enhance the scene. Early-flowering species are by now fading as their petals fall and their fruits form from the swelling lower part of the flower head.

Arrowhead

Flowering rush

*Pink flowers
on stalks*

Developing fru

RUSH IN BLOOM
The dark pink blooms
flowering rush are carried
stems up to 5 ft (1.5 m) tal
As explained on page 32 t
is not a true rush, though
leaves are rushlike and
grow in a rosette from the
stem base. It is often plan
to decorate ornamental
ponds.

Common figwort

FROTHY FLOWER
Meadowsweet's tiny, creamy
flowers combine to form a
foamy mass carried on a firm
stem, often more than 3 ft
(1 m) tall. This relative of the
rose likes pond sides, boggy
areas, and wet meadows.

GROWN UP
The figwort shown on
page 10 has now grown
to its full height of almost
3 ft (1 m). The flowers
are spaced at regular
intervals on the upper
section of stem.

FRUITS FORMING
The water arum's fruits a
ripening as the specialize
cup-shaped leaves aroun
them, called spathes,
begin to yellow and with
(see also p. 10).

Spathe

*Develop
fruits*

Mass of tiny flowers

Meadowsweet

Water arum

*Dark-green leaves
have notched edges*

*Figwort's stem has
a distinctive square
cross section*

GRAYISH-GREEN SHEEN
Osier, a typically water-loving willow, has extremely long, sharply pointed leaves. The tiny hairs on the underside of each leaf give it a grayish-green sheen.

Osier

Hawthorn

Haw

Water plantain's small pinky-white flowers bloom on tall, erect sprays of stems at this time of year (p. 57)

Dark green upperside of leaf

Gray underside of leaf

GREEN TO RED
Hawthorns tolerate wide variations in soil type and moisture content, so this tree is often found growing by ponds. The green fruits are called "haws." In a few weeks the haws will turn a deep rich, red color and attract birds such as waxwings and tits to the pond side.

THERED PETALS
e bright blooms (p. 11) of the low flag iris have withered to wn, and the fruit capsules are w forming. Each capsule embles a chunky pea pod and ntains several knobbly seeds.

Seed pods

ST.-JOHN'S-WORT
This plant (see also p. 16) grows in damp places such as shady woods and pond banks. The flowers begin to fade in midsummer.

St.-John's-wort

SPHERES AND SPEARS
Its yellow flower indicates that greater spearwort is a type of buttercup. Two round, spiky heads of ripening fruits are shown, as well as the spear-shaped leaves that give the plant its name.

Ripening fruit

Withered flower

Yellow flag

PINK FORGET-ME-NOT
Water forget-me-not flowers throughout the summer, in damp and shady places. Its stems trail along the pond edge, and its flowers may be blue, white, or pink.

Spear-shaped leaves

Water forget-me-not

Greater spearwort

15

Midsummer animals

MIDSUMMER IS A TIME OF GROWTH and departure in the pond. The frantic spring and early-summer rush of new life is slowing down. The surviving youngsters of this year's eggs, now few in number, settle down to the serious business of growing, building up sto of fat in their bodies, and preparing for the shorter, colder days ahead. Frog and toad tadpoles have changed into air-breathing mini-adults, ready to leave the water and take their first hops on land. A few young newts may stay as tadpoles with gills through the coming autumn and winter, but others, now adult in shape, are also moving away. The departure from the pond continues as aquatic insect larvae of many kinds develop into adults (p. 50), from tiny gnats, midges, and mosquitoes to the mighty dragonflies (p. 48) that prey on them.

Tiny gnats (male and female) dance above the pond's surface during long summer evenings

Not rowing but flying, this water boatman shows its strong wings (p. 51)

Toadlet

Newtlets

Gills

Toadlet

Water snail

Growth rings

RINGS AND BANDS
Periods of slow growth are visible on this water snail's shell. They are the thin rings toward the opening which cross the spiral banding pattern.

NEWTLETS
These young newts still have their gills to help absorb oxygen from the warm summe pond water. They hide among weeds, eating water fleas and other tiny creatures

TOADLETS
By now, toad tadpoles have grown their front legs and lost their tails, to resemble their parents. In midsummer they leave the pond for life on land.

HAPPY WANDERER
The wandering snail is more tolerant of water with fewer minerals (p. 52) than, for example, the great pond snail is - and so is more widespread in ponds and slow rivers.

BABY BIVALVES
In about 10 years, these young freshwater mollusks will be many times this size (p. 52). In their early years they are busy feeding and absorbing calcium from the water to build their shell.

Young freshwater mollusks

Wandering snails

Snail emerging from shell

SQUARE STEM
There are several species of St.-John's-wort (p. 15). This one is square-stemmed, and lines watersides, marshes, and damp shrubland.

Square-stemmed St.-John's-wort

CARNIVORE PARADE
These five fearsome-looking insect larvae prey on any small creatures they can overpower in the pond. Acilius and Hydaticus will become diving beetles; the other three will turn into dragonflies.

Acilius beetle larva

Hawker nymph

Hydaticus beetle larva

Hawker nymph

Darter nymph

HUNTING ADULT
Last year's dragonfly nymph is now adult, patrolling the air space above the pond and hunting small flyers like the gnats opposite.

Golden-ringed dragonfly

DARTER NYMPH
The nymphs (p. 48) of darter dragonflies have shorter bodies than those of hawker dragonflies, making them look a little like spiders.

FLYING SKATERS
Pond skaters belong to the "hemipteran," or bug group. They have sharp piercing mouthparts that suck the body fluids from their prey. These agile insects can skate, jump, and fly (p. 51).

Pond skaters

LEAF DAMAGE
By midsummer these water hawthorn leaves have been damaged by insects and other aquatic plant-eaters. The white-petaled flowers are now in bloom (bottom right).

The water stick insect is another predator of small aquatic creatures (p. 51)

A few mayflies are still about in mid to late summer (p. 50)

Baby stickleback

Baby stickleback

Water hawthorn

Adult male stickleback

PARENT AND OFFSPRING
By summer, the adult male stickleback has lost his red-throated breeding colors (pp. 9 and 25) and become dull and unnoticeable. The smaller fish are young sticklebacks, born in the spring.

The pond in autumn

GRADUALLY THE SUMMER ENDS and the hours of daylight shorten. Although the sun's rays may still be warm in midafternoon, the nights are increasingly chilly.
Autumn has arrived, and pond wildlife is slowing down and preparing for winter. Summer-visiting birds have departed, but their place is taken by waterfowl such as the brent goose, Bewick swan, and pintail duck (p. 28), which fly in from their far-north breeding grounds to enliven larger ponds, lakes, and marshes. Mammals and resident birds feed greedily on the ripe fruits, building up their fat stores for the winter. However, their shelters and hiding places are gradually being whittled away as the cold wind rattles crackly brown leaves from their stems, making the pond's banks look bare and untidy.

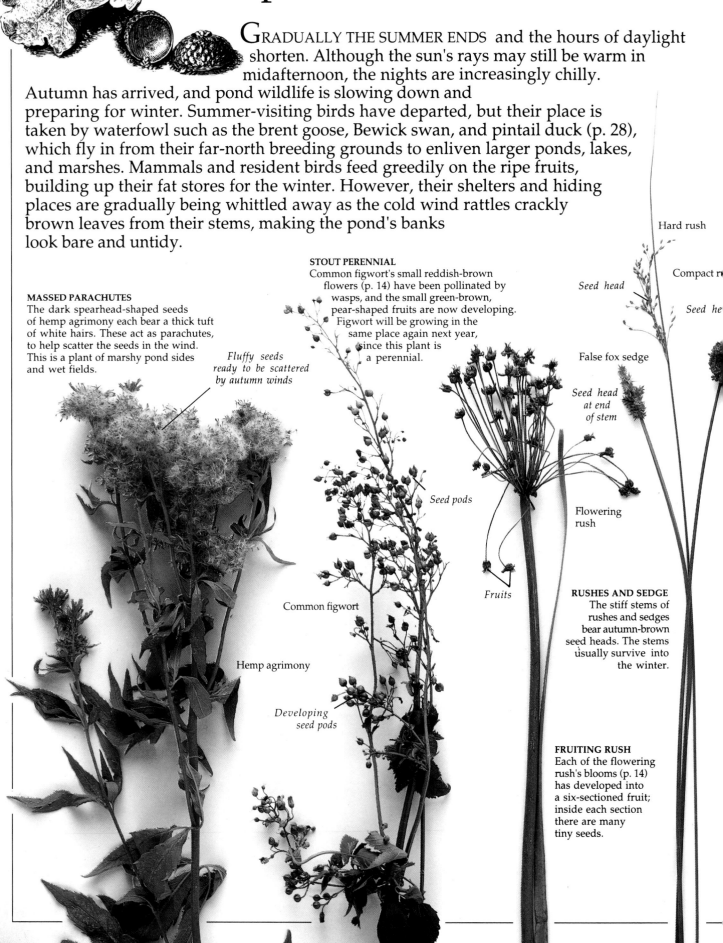

MASSED PARACHUTES
The dark spearhead-shaped seeds of hemp agrimony each bear a thick tuft of white hairs. These act as parachutes, to help scatter the seeds in the wind. This is a plant of marshy pond sides and wet fields.

Fluffy seeds ready to be scattered by autumn winds

STOUT PERENNIAL
Common figwort's small reddish-brown flowers (p. 14) have been pollinated by wasps, and the small green-brown, pear-shaped fruits are now developing. Figwort will be growing in the same place again next year, since this plant is a perennial.

Seed pods

Hard rush

Seed head

Compact r

Seed he

False fox sedge

Seed head at end of stem

Flowering rush

Fruits

Common figwort

Hemp agrimony

Developing seed pods

RUSHES AND SEDGE
The stiff stems of rushes and sedges bear autumn-brown seed heads. The stems usually survive into the winter.

FRUITING RUSH
Each of the flowering rush's blooms (p. 14) has developed into a six-sectioned fruit; inside each section there are many tiny seeds.

WINTER POKER
Reed mace's familiar brown "poker" of seeds stands guard over marshes and ponds, usually throughout the winter. In spring the poker bursts to scatter the fluffy-haired seeds.

Brown "poker" full of seeds

SNAILS SLOWING DOWN
Falling water temperatures mean that even pond snails begin to move around more slowly, tending to stay in deeper water.

Pond snails

Caddis fly cases

Alder cones

Reed mace

Newtlet

Dragonfly nymph

HOME IN A TUBE
Rectangular leaf fragments stuck into a spiral pattern and curled into a tube signal the larval case of the great red sedge, a type of caddis fly (p. 50). These larvae will emerge as adult flies next year.

NEXT YEAR'S ADULT
Dragonfly nymphs found in the pond at this time of year will survive the winter and emerge next year.

AUTUMN JUVENILE
A young common newt, still equipped with gills, will spend the winter as a "juvenile" and finish its change into an adult next year.

Alder

ALDER "CONES"
In autumn the alder's green fruits ripen to a brown-black color and stay on the tree during winter. They are sometimes mistaken for small pine cones, but the alder is not a conifer. It prefers pond banks and the sides of streams, and its light seeds drop onto the water and float to new ground.

Seed pods

Yellow flag

RECYCLING FUNGI
Animal and plant corpses are digested by fungi, and their nutrients are recycled. Here, an old pond-side tree was attacked and weakened by bracket fungi.

Bracket fungi grow on the outside of the trunk

ON THE BOTTOM
Leaves, twigs, and other debris blow into the pond or are washed in by heavy autumn rains. This heap of debris, lying over the mud of the pond bed, will shelter all kinds of small water creatures during the winter months.

SOON TO SET SEED
The seed capsules of the yellow flag iris are now thick with ripening brown seeds (compare the same "pods" on p. 15). Eventually the fleshy capsule walls dry out and split into three boat-shaped segments; these peel back to release the seeds.

Oak leaf

Willow leaf

Birch leaf

Willow twigs

The pond in winter

WHERE DO FLIES GO IN THE WINTER? More to the point, where do pond snails, flatworms, aquatic larvae, fish, amphibians and other pond creatures go in the winter? There are several strategies for surviving the season of cold and ice. "Cold-blooded" animals can generally live in the coldest water, as long as they ar not trapped in solid ice. Fish, and some water insects, mollusks, and worms, move to the deepest part of the pond to avoid being iced in. As the water cools, they do too, and their bodies need less and less energy, so they can survive with hardly any food. Cold water holds more dissolved oxygen than warm water; and supplies are enriched by various types of waterweeds, which can carry out photosynthesis (p. 46) using the frosty sunlight that penetrates the layer of ice. Coupled with the reduced needs of the inactive animals, this means there are sufficient supplies of oxygen for life even when the pond is iced over for days. Another strategy, adopted by many very small water creatures, is to lay eggs in the autumn; the adults die and the eggs hatch next spring. Amphibians, such as frogs and toads, sleep through the winter in a sheltered place on land.

Water lily leaf

Common re

LAST REMAINS
Water lily and arrowhead leaves still bear their long, anchoring stems - but the leaves are now browned, tattered and torn by waves, wind, and frost.

POND SKATERS
Humans are active above, and animals and plants spend the winter below.

WIND-BURNED REED
Common reed flower heads stubbornly resist winter's gales and snowstorms. Even the leaves stay stuck to the stems, though the combined effects of frost and windblasting turn them to crinkly brown ribbons.

Arrowhead leaf

Old leaves are evidence of the trees that grow around the pond

BLANKETS OF LEAVES
Decay is slow in the icy water. Shed leaves settle in blanket- like layers, which protect and insulate the small creatures and the winter buds of plants sandwiched between them.

THIS YEAR, NEXT YEAR
The alder's greenery has now disappeared (p. 19), leaving the woody "cones" to rattle on the bare twigs. However, renewed growth is already signaled by next year's smaller, paler, developing catkins.

Alder

Next year's catkins developing

This year's cones

WINTER WEEPING
Slender, leafless willow twigs hang over the pond, rattling in the breeze and easily shedding snow to keep them from cracking under its weight.

Bittersweet

END OF THE SEASON
One of our seasonal markers, the yellow flag iris, is now a brown and tattered remnant of its former green-and-yellow glory. Only the leaves persist; but new life is just around the corner.

Weeping willow twig

Red berries are poisonous

A TOUCH OF SCARLET
Bittersweet trails through the bank vegetation, its bright red berries adding a touch of color to the winter landscape. Beware its attraction, though - the berries are poisonous.

Yellow flag

Sheet of ice lifted from shallow pond

ICE IS NICE
Strangely, a blanket of ice is no bad thing for pond inhabitants. Ice is a good insulator, so while temperatures may plunge far below freezing in the winds above, down in the pond's depths the water is a bearable few degrees above freezing.

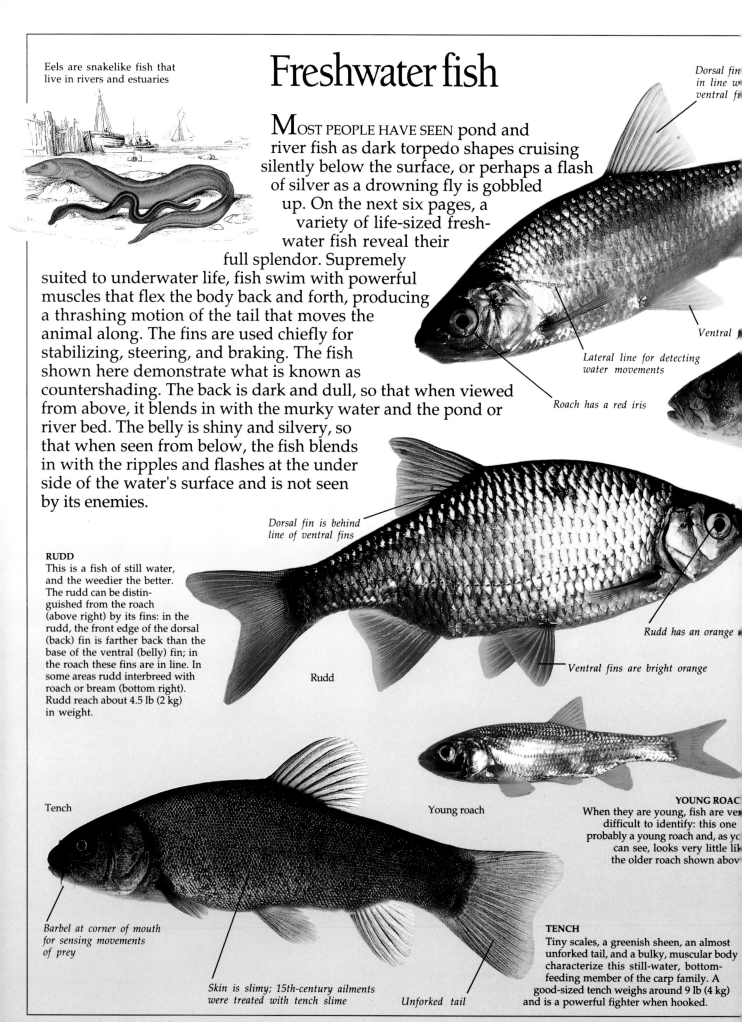

Eels are snakelike fish that live in rivers and estuaries

Freshwater fish

MOST PEOPLE HAVE SEEN pond and river fish as dark torpedo shapes cruising silently below the surface, or perhaps a flash of silver as a drowning fly is gobbled up. On the next six pages, a variety of life-sized freshwater fish reveal their full splendor. Supremely suited to underwater life, fish swim with powerful muscles that flex the body back and forth, producing a thrashing motion of the tail that moves the animal along. The fins are used chiefly for stabilizing, steering, and braking. The fish shown here demonstrate what is known as countershading. The back is dark and dull, so that when viewed from above, it blends in with the murky water and the pond or river bed. The belly is shiny and silvery, so that when seen from below, the fish blends in with the ripples and flashes at the under side of the water's surface and is not seen by its enemies.

Dorsal fin
in line w
ventral f

Ventral

Lateral line for detecting
water movements

Roach has a red iris

Dorsal fin is behind
line of ventral fins

RUDD
This is a fish of still water, and the weedier the better. The rudd can be distinguished from the roach (above right) by its fins: in the rudd, the front edge of the dorsal (back) fin is farther back than the base of the ventral (belly) fin; in the roach these fins are in line. In some areas rudd interbreed with roach or bream (bottom right). Rudd reach about 4.5 lb (2 kg) in weight.

Rudd

Rudd has an orange

Ventral fins are bright orange

Tench

Young roach

YOUNG ROAC
When they are young, fish are ve
difficult to identify: this one
probably a young roach and, as yo
can see, looks very little lik
the older roach shown abov

Barbel at corner of mouth
for sensing movements
of prey

Skin is slimy; 15th-century ailments
were treated with tench slime

Unforked tail

TENCH
Tiny scales, a greenish sheen, an almost unforked tail, and a bulky, muscular body characterize this still-water, bottom-feeding member of the carp family. A good-sized tench weighs around 9 lb (4 kg) and is a powerful fighter when hooked.

ROACH

The roach is a common, widespread fish that can live in clear rivers or muddy, mildly polluted canals. It is an unfussy eater, taking both plant and animal food. Roach are somewhat similar to rudd (below left) and dace. They live for about 10 years, and the largest grow to 4.5 lb (2 kg) in weight.

oach

SALMON BYPASS

On its way upriver to spawn, a big salmon can leap 10 ft (3 m) out of the water to clear waterfalls and other obstacles. But weirs, locks, and dams have increased the number of hazards. One answer is the man-made salmon "ladder," which the fish can leap in easy stages.

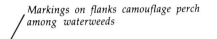
Markings on flanks camouflage perch among waterweeds

Dark spot on spiny dorsal fin

Perch

SALMON

The "king of fish" hatches in gravelly, fast-flowing water. It spends the first three or so years of its life in a river and is known as a "parr" (resembling the trout parr on p. 27). It then migrates to the sea, becoming more silvery and known as a "smolt." After one to four years feeding on small fish and crustaceans at sea, mature adults return to the river of their birth to spawn. Most then die. The biggest salmon are over 3 ft (1 m) long and weigh 55 lbs (25 kg) or more.

Engraving of an adult salmon shows how the tail is thrashed from side to side to provide power for leaping out of the water

ERCH

he five or so dark vertical bars on e perch's flanks, the two dorsal fins the front one with prominent spines - nd the reddish ventral and anal fins ake the perch an exceptionally andsome fish. This youngster f one to two years may eigh 4.5 lb (2 kg) when fully grown. erch feed on worms, crustaceans, ollusks, insects, and small fish.

Ventral fins are tinged orange

Lateral line

Dorsal fin

BREAM

Deep-bodied, large-scaled bream live in still and slow-flowing waters. They feed on small water animals such as insect larvae, and some water plants. The largest bream can grow up to 2.5 ft (80 cm) long and weigh about 10 lb (4.5 kg).

The "stripe" along a fish's side, showing especially clearly here, is the lateral line. It is a groove of specialized tissues that detect vibrations in the water, in effect allowing the fish to "hear" and "feel" water movements.

Deeply forked tail

Group of bream

*Distinctive markings make
these fish highly prized*

Koi carp

*Mouth can be exten
to suck up food f
pond bot*

Barbel on side of mou

KOI CARP

People in Japan and China have been breeding carp
for hundreds of years. The koi is a cultivated variety of fish
belonging to the same group as the common carp. It is
known in Japan as Nishiki Koi, or Brocaded Carp. Koi have
been bred for their color and patterning as well as for size - some
grow to over 3 ft (1 m) long. They have been stocked in ponds and lakes
across Europe and North America, and prized specimens are extremely valuable.

PIKE AND EEL

An account from the 1880s describes a pike of some 10 lb (4.5 kg)
that attempted to swallow an eel weighing almost as much. The
eel tried to wriggle out through the pike's gills, the pike bit it in
two, and both perished. Although the truth of this story is a
little doubtful, it illustrates the voracious nature of the pike, a
sleek predator with a mouthful of sharp teeth, and shows the
toughness of the eel, which wriggles furiously and throws off
slime when in trouble.
Female eels grow to 3 ft
(1 m) long and weigh
around 4.5 lb (2 kg);
males may be half this
size.

Large, reflecting scales

Mirror carp

MIRROR CARP

Another form of common carp is the mirror carp, so named
from the unusually large, shiny scales. These may occur
down the side of the body (sometimes following the lateral line),
and perhaps along the back, or scattered at random. Like other
carp it feeds on the bottom, consuming small aquatic creatures
and water plants. It reaches weights of up to 20 lb (9 kg).

Parts of the body have no sca

BITTERLING

Resembling a miniature crucian carp in shape, the bitterling is an attractive little fish that is full-grown at about 3 in (8 cm) long. It lives in ponds, lakes, and slow rivers, eating small water creatures and plants. It has a unique method of spawning. In late spring the female develops a long tube, through which she lays her eggs in a freshwater mussel such as a swan mussel (p. 52). The male releases his sperm nearby, which is sucked in by the mussel and fertilizes the eggs. The eggs develop and hatch inside the mussel, and young "fry" leave their host after about three weeks, when their yolk sacs have been consumed.

...ue flash identifies the bitterling

...ort lateral line

...tterling

STICKLEBACK NEST

In late spring the male stickleback makes a nest of plant pieces. He dances back and forth in a zig zag to attract a female, who lays her eggs in the nest. He fertilizes them, and next day entices another female. After several egg batches have been laid, he guards them until they hatch.

Adult has very deep body

Overlapping scales can be golden, bronze, or olive-green

Crucian carp

CRUCIAN CARP

A relative of the common carp, the crucian is very tolerant of water that is low in oxygen. It inhabits
...eedy, stagnating, ponds and lakes, canals, reservoirs, and slow
...vers. An average adult is 1 ft (30 cm) long and weighs 10 oz
...80 gm), although record breakers of more than 4.5 lb (2 kg)
...ave been hooked. It has a deeper body than the common carp
...d lacks the single pair of barbels (small "feelers") on the side
... the mouth.

Grass carp

GRASS CARP

This plant-eating, golden-colored fish is a native of China and Russia and has been introduced into many waterways to control weed growth. In their native habitat they can grow up to 75 lb (35 kg) in weight, although introduced specimens are usually around 9 lb (4 kg).

...rbels on
...outh

...UDGEON

...e carnivorous gudgeon
...ubs about on the bottom using
... two barbels to locate its food of
...orms, insect larvae, and other small
...ater creatures. It rarely grows to more
...an 6 in (15 cm). Schools (groups) of gudgeon are common
... rivers, especially in the middle sections; they also
...ve in lakes and canals.

Spots on dorsal side

Speckled, translucent fins

Gudgeon

The trout

FEW FRESHWATER FISH match the trout for natural beauty and grace, for fighting power when hooked - and for taste when cooked! Trout belong to the salmon family. The brown trout and the sea trout are, in fact, different forms of the same species. The brown trout lives all its life in fresh water; the sea trout feeds in the sea and enters its home stream in summer, to breed in autumn. Adult brown trout may reach 3 ft (1 m) in length; sea trout can be half as long again. There are many variations between these two forms, telling them apart is difficult, because sea trout darken when they have been in fresh water for a few weeks and look like brown trout. In any case, trout differ greatly in appearance, depending on where they live, the nature of the water, the type of stream or lake bed, and the food they eat. Rainbow trout are another trout species altogether.

TYPICAL TROUT COUNTRY
An ideal trout stream - clear and cool running water, high in dissolved oxygen, with a gravelly bed for spawning. Trout are also found in clean lakes, usually in the shallows near their food.

Lateral line

Movements of the very mobile pectoral fins enable the fish to swim upward or downward

STREAMLINED PREDATOR
Brown trout, like other trout, are carnivorous. Food varies from tiny water fleas, flies, aquatic insect larvae (such as caddis larvae) and freshwater shrimps, to shellfish and other mollusks. The big brown trout, from large, deep lakes, prey on other fish such as char or whitefish.

Brown trout

COLORS OF THE RAINBOW
Rainbow trout were originally found in western North America (especially California). Like the brown trout, there are sea, lake, and river forms. Their eggs were brought to Europe in the 1900s, and these fish have since been introduced into many rivers, reservoirs, and lakes to provide sport and food. Rainbow trout breed in some large reservoirs, but rivers have to be regularly stocked with young produced in hatcheries (trout farms). The rainbow trout can live in warmer, less oxygenated water than the brown trout, so they are stocked in small lakes and large ponds where the brown trout would probably not survive.

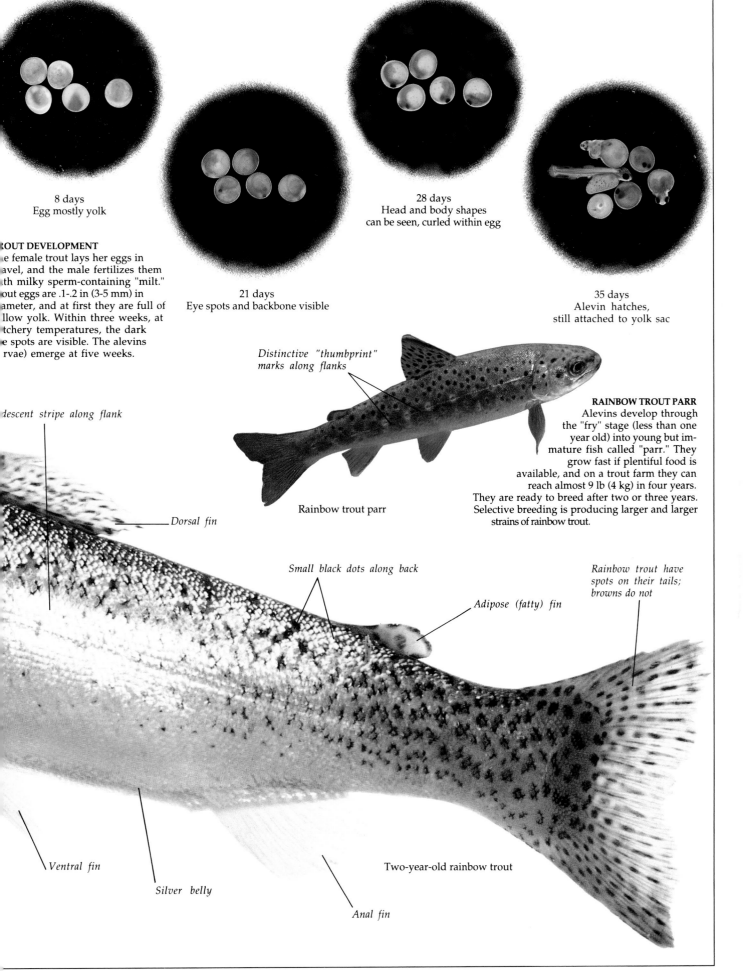

8 days
Egg mostly yolk

21 days
Eye spots and backbone visible

28 days
Head and body shapes
can be seen, curled within egg

35 days
Alevin hatches,
still attached to yolk sac

TROUT DEVELOPMENT
The female trout lays her eggs in
gravel, and the male fertilizes them
with milky sperm-containing "milt."
Trout eggs are .1-.2 in (3-5 mm) in
diameter, and at first they are full of
yellow yolk. Within three weeks, at
hatchery temperatures, the dark
eye spots are visible. The alevins
(larvae) emerge at five weeks.

Distinctive "thumbprint"
marks along flanks

RAINBOW TROUT PARR
Alevins develop through
the "fry" stage (less than one
year old) into young but immature fish called "parr." They
grow fast if plentiful food is
available, and on a trout farm they can
reach almost 9 lb (4 kg) in four years.
They are ready to breed after two or three years.
Selective breeding is producing larger and larger
strains of rainbow trout.

Rainbow trout parr

Iridescent stripe along flank

Dorsal fin

Small black dots along back

Adipose (fatty) fin

Rainbow trout have
spots on their tails;
browns do not

Ventral fin

Silver belly

Anal fin

Two-year-old rainbow trout

27

Waterfowl

WATER AND ITS RESIDENT WILDLIFE attract an amazing variety of birds. Quite at home on ponds, lakes, and rivers (as well as seashores) across the world are about 150 species of wildfowl, including swans, geese, and ducks. These generally heavy-bodied birds have webbed feet for swimming and long, flexible necks for dabbling in the water and rummaging in the muddy bed for food. During spring, dense plant growth on the bank provides many species with safe and sheltered nesting sites. In summer, the proud parents can be seen leading their fluffy chicks across the water. Aquatic plants and animals are a ready source of food for most of the year. In winter, when ponds freeze over, many wildfowl retreat to parks and gardens where they feast on scraps donated by well-wishing humans. Others fly south, often covering vast distances to find a more favorable climate in which to spend the winter.

Teal nest and eggs

Eider duck nest and eggs

Soft down feathers insulate the eggs in the nest

SPECIALLY GROWN DOWN
Ultra-soft eiderdown feathers grow on the female eider duck's breast. She plucks them to cocoon her eggs as she nests on seashore, lake shore or riverbank.

TEAL NEST
The teal makes its n in dense undergrowth The female is very careful when visiting her chicks, so as not to attract predators.

TUFTED DUCK EGG
The six to 14 eggs are laid in a nes close to the water's edge. The chi hatches after 25 days in the egg, and within a day it is swimming.

Teal, one of the
smallest ducks

*Nest would be
lined with down
when being used*

ON THE WING
All wildfowl are strong
flyers, many covering
vast distances during
their annual migration.

Vane

Quill

Flight feathers

Pintail
wing

ECLIPSE
Out of the breeding season,
the pintail drake molts to
his unnoticeable "eclipse"
plumage, which looks like the
female's coloring.

MALE AND FEMALE
In the breeding
season, most male
ducks, like the pintail
(far right), have bright
plumage to catch the
female's eye. The
female (right) is duller,
for camouflage on the nest.

Tufted duck

PARTIAL TO MUSSELS
The tufted duck feeds on freshwater
mussels, as well as small fish, frogs,
and insects.

Tufted duck
skull

MUSCOVY DUCK
This native of Central and South
American ponds and marshes has
a broad bill that scoops up aquatic
plants and animals alike.

Muscovy duck

Muscovy duck
skull

BEWARE THE ORANGE BILL
The mute swan's bill is usually covered by an
orange sheath. Male swans can be extremely
vicious, particularly in the breeding season when
defending their territory.

Swan

*The broad bill shape is
suitable for dabbling
for plants in the water*

FROM THE MOLT
Water-dwelling birds depend on
their feathers to keep them dry
and much time is spent
preening to keep the feathers
in good condition.

Mute swan skull

Water birds

A STRETCH OF WATER acts as a magnet for all types of bird life. Many species, from sparrows to pheasants, come to drink. Others come to feed, from the tall, elegant heron that stands motionless as it watches for prey, to the flash of shimmering blue that signifies a kingfisher diving for its dinner. Bank plants, floating and submerged waterweeds, fish, frogs, insect larvae, shellfish, and other aquatic life provide food for many birds. Some species, like reed buntings and warblers, find security in the dense reed beds and waterside vegetation. Here they nest and raise their chicks, safe from predators such as foxes and hawks.

Kingfisher wing

Kingfisher

THE EXPERT FISHER
The brilliantly colored kingfisher dives from its favorite perch for fish, tadpoles, and shellfish. The sword-shaped bill is ideal for stabbing or spearing fish, then holding the slippery prey until it can be beaten into stillness on a branch and swallowed headfirst.

The white eggs have a glossy surface

Kingfisher eggs

WHITE EGGS
Kingfishers nest in a streambank burrow up to 3 ft (1 m) long, so their eggs are white - there is no need for camouflaging colors.

KINGFISHER WING AND TAIL
The electric colors act as a warning to predatory birds, advertising that the flesh is foul-tasting.

Tail and wing markings vary from species to species

Short wings beat rapidly when flying

Kingfisher tail

Kingfisher skull

Sharp bill for stabbing fish

Heron

LONG AND LANKY
Herons inhabit ponds, marshes, and rivers, stalking fish and frogs in the shallows.

Long, sharp bill for spearing fish

Heron skull

HERON'S HARPOON
The heron's fearsome bill makes an excellent fish-stabbing spear. This bird stands patiently until prey comes within reach, then darts out its long neck, stabs the victim, tosses it around, and swallows it whole.

Bittern skull

BITTERN
This bird points its bill skyward and sways with the reeds to avoid detection. It can also climb up reed stems. The bittern builds a shallow platform of reed leaves and stalks hidden deep in the reed beds. The five to six eggs take four weeks to hatch.

STEALTHY STALKER
The bittern is a solitary, daytime feeder, using its pointed beak to catch frogs, small fish, and insects.

Reed warbler
nest

Reed warbler

*Nest is made from reed
flower heads and
other vegetation*

SNIPE EGG
The coloring
camouflages the eggs
in the nest of this
small wading bird.

LITTLE GREBE EGG
White when laid,
eggs get discolored
by plants and mud.
The little grebe is
also known as the
"dabchick."

WATER RAIL EGG
Water rails are shy
birds of waterside
undergrowth. There
can be as many as
15 eggs in a clutch.

*Nest is woven
round reed stalks*

HERON EGG
The blue eggs are laid
in well-defended nests
built of sticks and
twigs.

Reed bunting

FINE RUSHWORK
The reed bunting's nest is
built by the female alone,
but both parents feed
the chicks on insects and
their larvae.

EEP CUP
he reed warbler's nest
supported by several
ems, usually of
ommon reed. Its cup is
xtra-deep, so that the
gs and chicks do not
ll out when high
inds blow the reeds
ver at an angle.

*The nest is made of
grasses and moss*

Reed bunting nest

Rushes and reeds

ALTHOUGH THEY LOOK quite similar, rushes and reeds are botanically very different. Sedges are often confused with rushes and reeds too. A rush is a grasslike plant with a round, usually solid stem and narrow, rigid leaves. A reed is a type of grass, usually tall, with feathery flower heads and the strap-like leaves typical of the grass family. A sedge is a grassy-looking plant but not a true grass; its stem is usually solid and triangular in section, unlike a grass's round, hollow stem. Despite their differences, these plants all have one thing in common - a liking for the wetness of marshes, pond edges, and riverbanks.

TINY FRUITS
The dark flower heads of the lesser pond sedge bear the tiny fruits called utricles.

Developing fruits

Hard rush

Loose cluster of tiny flowers

HARD RUSH
Rushes are related to lilies, but their smaller, wind-pollinated flowers could not be more different.

Common reed stalk and leaves

Stalk remains standing in winter as a hard cane

Lesser pond sedge

NOT A RUSH
Despite its name and appearance, the flowering rush is not a true rush. Its name probably comes from its tall, rushlike stem and leaves, and the fact that it grows in the same habitat as true rushes.

Flowering rush

Rose-pink flowers grow on leafless stalks

Rushlike leaves

REED WEED
The common reed grows almost too well in virtually any damp area, from slightly salty places near the coast to marshy areas and the banks of ponds, lakes, and slow-flowing rivers. It stands up to 10 ft (3 m) tall and is considered a weed in some water-ways (p. 34).

32

Male flowers release clouds of pollen

Ten to 20 male flower heads

Branched bur reed

Female flowers are fertilized by wind-carried pollen from male flowers, and fluffy seeds are released when the flower head splits open

Two to four female flower heads

Male and female flowers in the same flower head

eat ed mace

BRANCHING OUT
Each stem of branched bur reed bears both male and female flowers. The smaller, ball-shaped ones toward the tip are male; the female ones are larger and spiky, like a rolled-up hedgehog.

False fox sedge

Triangular stem has sharp edges if rubbed downward

FALSE FOX SEDGE
On top of sharp-edged stems sit the tufty, yellow-green flower heads containing both male and female flowers.

Branched bur reed

TWO HEADS IN ONE
The great reed mace's poker-shaped flower head is in two parts. Above are hundreds of golden pollen-bearing male organs, and below are thousands of tiny female flowers packed into the brown cigar shape. The whole resembles the mace, a weapon of 15th-century knights, hence the name. The plant is commonly, but wrongly, called the bulrush, after the paintings of *Moses in the Bulrushes* (p. 35).

Flower stalk

Bract at base of each branch of flower stalk

The reed bed

THE REED BED IS THE SILENT INVADER OF OPEN WATER. Dense growths of tall, marsh-ground plants, such as reed mace and common reed, spread around the pond's edge by thick underground rhizomes (stems). These grow sideways through the mud toward the water and send up fresh shoots at intervals. They spread into the shallows, pushing aside water lilies and mare's-tails. The reed stems slow the movement of water and trap particles carried by the current. At the end of each season the old leaves, stems, and fruits add to the growing tangle. In a few years, previously open water can be turned into thickly vegetated marsh. Some years later the reed bed has moved on, still swallowing up the shallows, and drier-ground plants such as osiers and sallows (types of willow) have moved in at the back of the bed. This conversion of water to land by characteristic stages is an example of "ecological succession."

Fool's watercress

WATER TO DRY LAND
Shown below are characteristic plants of pond and lake edge, with sallows and sedges higher up the shore, reed beds toward the middle, and mare's-tails and long-stemmed lilies in deeper water. As the reeds spread and invade the water, this becomes clogged and marshy and, over the years, the whole pattern of plant growth moves toward the center of the pond. Of course, this does not happen in all bodies of water. People clear or harvest the reeds, and storms, flood currents, plant diseases, and hungry animals keep a natural balance.

Dry land

Marshy area

Shallow water

Open water

Horizontal stems

A REED ROOF OVER THEIR HEADS
The strong, long-wearing reeds are used as roofing material in many regions, from huts in Egypt and Sudan, to houses on stilts in Indonesia and wooden cabins in southern North America. The English thatch style (above) repels rain and insulates at the same time. A skilled thatcher working with quality reeds can make a roof that remains weatherproof for 40 years or more.

CREEPING CRESS
The fool's watercress gets its name because its leaves resemble true watercress. It is found in large quantities at the back of many reed beds, and its horizontal, straggling stems add to the general tangle of vegetation.

READY FOR RECYCLING
The thick, black mud of reed-bed areas is rich in decaying plant and animal remains. Its nutrients are soon recycled by the rushes, reeds, and other plants.

Reed-bed mud

Underground rhizome

Sweet flag

Long straight stalks

Flower head may be 8 ft (2.5 m) above the roots

Dark-greeen leaves have pale undersides

Osier shoot

EARLY HARVEST
The reed cutter's season is usually the tail end of winter and early spring. Last year's stems are cut near the base before this year's shoots emerge, which ensures a future harvest.

THICK AND FLESHY
The juicy, strap-shaped leaves of sweet flag sprout from a thick horizontal stem. The stem has many small roots that hold the marshy mud together.

MOSES IN THE . . . ?
As a baby, Moses was supposedly hidden in a basket in a reed bed on the bank of the Nile River in Egypt. Illustrations showing this are titled *Moses in the Bulrushes* although most versions portray the baby in a clump of reed mace. This confusion has led to the name "bulrush" being given to reed mace (p. 33); the true bulrush is somewhat similar to the spike rush.

The thin leaves dry very quickly when picked

Top of common reed stem

WILLOWS FOR WEAVING
Osiers are found at the back of reed beds, on less marshy ground. They have long, straight shoots and a shrubby shape. They are often coppiced (cut at ground level) to provide flexible stems ("withes") for woven chairs and baskets.

THE STRAIGHT AND NARROW
The straight, narrow stems of common reed are ideal thatching material. They are also used to make paper and other pulp-based products. Plant growth in reed beds is often very fast because there is plenty of water and nutrients, and the slender stems and leaves allow light to reach the lower levels.

Base of common reed stem

Waterside mammals

Freshwater habitats, from rivers and streams to the marshy edges of lakes and ponds, provide a home and food for a number of mammals. All the "aquatic" mammals shown here have fur coats adapted to their watery habitat. The fur of a mink, for example, is of two main types. Long, thick, flattened "guard hairs" provide physical protection and camouflaging coloration. For each guard hair there are 20 or more softer hairs of the underfur, only half as long, which trap air to keep water out and body heat in. The owners sensibly spend much time combing and cleaning their fur, keeping it in tip-top condition. Another adaptation for watery life is webs between the toes, for more efficient swimming.

FURRY FORAGER
The water shrew's dark-furred body is only about 3 in (8 cm) long. This bustling insect-eater often lives in a bankside system of narrow tunnels that press water from its coat as it squeezes through. It eats small fish, water insects, and even frogs, and hunts on dry land for worms and other small creatures.

Mink

ADAPTABLE CARNIVORE
Minks are less specialized hunters than otters and, besides fish, will eat birds, aquatic insects, and land animals such as rabbits. The broad, webbed back feet provide the main swimming power.

American mink skull

Canine teeth

Molar teeth

TEARERS AND CUTTERS
The mink's four long canine teeth, toward the front of its mouth, are built for catching prey and tearing flesh. The molars, at the back, are ridged for cutting.

TOOTHLESS "BEAK"
When a baby platypus hatches it has teeth, but these are soon lost. Adults grind up the food of shellfish, water insects, and worms using horny plates along their jaws.

Platypus

Platypus skull

Long bill for grinding food

DUCK'S BILL, MAMMAL'S FUR
The Australian platypus, a monotreme (egg-laying mammal), has a "bill" covered with leathery, sensitive skin. The bill is its only means of finding food - by touch - as it forages in muddy creek beds. It closes its eyes and ears when diving.

LODGE IN THE RIVER
A beaver family lives in a semi-submerged mud-and-stick house called a "lodge." The beavers build a dam of branches, twigs, stones, and mud across the stream, which raises the local water level and isolates the lodge for safety. During winter they swim under the ice to a "deep freezer" food store of woody stems and twigs.

Lodge

Mud-and-stick walls

Living chamber (above water)

Food store

Raised water level

Entrance (under water)

Da[m]

ng canine teeth
grasping fish

Otter skull

ATCHFUL SWIMMER
ostrils, eyes, and ears are
aced high on the head
that the otter can
im almost
bmerged yet still
eathe, look,
d listen.

HUNTING THE OTTER
Otter hunting was once considered a sport and still occurs in
some places, although in many countries this animal is now
protected by law. Today these creatures are also at risk from
pollution and from development of waterways for fishing
and boating.

E GAME OF LIFE
ters spend much
ne at play, either
their own or with
e another. Such "games"
ay help to sharpen hunting
ills.

*Molar teeth for
grinding food*

ENORMOUS GNAWERS
The beaver's large
chisel-like front teeth
(typical of rodents) can
gnaw through tree trunks
with ease.

TURE'S LOGGERS
avers cut down trees for food
d also to build homes in lakes
ey create for themselves
elow left). They eat
terweeds, leaves,
d other plant
atter.

Beaver skull

*Large incisor teeth
for gnawing*

Beaver

FLAT SLAP
The beaver's tail is flattened and scaly. Besides its use
as a rudder and paddle, it can be slapped on the
water's surface to warn other beavers of danger.

aver tail

Frogs, toads, and newts

AMPHIBIANS ARE ANIMALS that never quite set themselves free of the water. As their name suggests (*amphi* for "both" and *bios* for "life"), they lead a double life: in the water when young, and out of it when adult. Many adult amphibians on land must stay in damp places so that they do not dry out. This is because some species "breathe" oxygen through the skin, as well as breathing it into their lungs, and only moist skin will absorb oxygen. Young amphibians just hatched from their eggs also absorb dissolved oxygen from the water through their skin, and in addition they have gills for breathing. Some amphibians, like the common frog and toad, prefer still water in which to breed. Others, such as the hellbender, a huge salamander from North America, frequent fast-flowing water. This may be because there is more dissolved oxygen in moving water than in still water, and such large amphibians need a bigger supply. Amphibians are divided into two main groups, distinguished by their tails: newts and salamanders have them, while frogs and toads do not (except as tadpoles).

Tiger salamander

STRUNG OUT
The common toad's spawn forms a black-speckled jelly necklace, 6 ft (2 m) or more long, wrapped around plant stems.

CLUMPED TOGETHER
Common frogs lay eggs (spawn) in clumps that float below the surface. Spawn from several females may collect in one large mass.

Common frog spawn

Developing tadpole

PATCHY PATTERNING
Common frogs vary in color, but in general they are mottled with patches of olive-green and brown.

Developing tadpole

Common toad spawn

Common toad

WARNING COLORATION
The vivid yellow and black blotchy pattern of the tiger salamander is thought to be a warning signal advising potential enemies that its skin and glands produce foul-tasting liquids.

Warning coloration

One-year-old common frog

Golden lined frog

Tympanum

GOLDEN LINED FROG
A frog's "ear" (tympanum) is a disk-shaped membrane behind its eye. That frogs have good hearing is indicated by the calls and croaks they use to communicate, especially when breeding.

Unwebbed front feet

Cuban tree frog

Rounded fingertips bear sticky pads

STICKY FINGER
This Cuban tree frog has rounded sticky pads on its digits, which help it grip leaves and twigs. Adults spend all their time in trees, leaving only to lay their eggs in a pond.

DRESSED IN GREEN
The startlingly green skin of Australia's dwarf tree frog hides it well among the bright leaves of its forest home.

Dwarf tree frog

GOING FOR A WALK
The squat, heavily built common toad prefers to move by walking in an unhurried fashion, though it can leap a short way when at risk. The "toes" are webbed, the "fingers" are not.

Mottled skin for camouflage

Webbed hind feet

GREEN TOAD
The green toad is smaller and slimmer than the common toad and can run surprisingly fast. It is often confused with the natterjack toad.

reen toad

ME TO GO
or spawning, atterjacks tend choose shallow, mporary pools. summer, crowds of adlets prepare to ave the water.

Natterjack toadlets

Natterjack spawn

Developing tadpole

NATTERJACK SPAWN
A single row of eggs is laid, entwined in pebbles or plant stems.

SUBMARINE HUNTER
The palmate newt spends part of the year on land, hibernating or feeding at night on worms and other small animals. It returns to the pond in spring to court and lay eggs.

Palmate newt

Mandarin newt

Warning coloration

A BIG EATER
All adult frogs and toads are carnivores. Big frogs have big mouths that can swallow large food items. There are several reliable reports of American bullfrogs eating bats!

American bullfrog

Developing newtlet

Newt eggs

SINGLE EGGS
Most newt species lay their eggs singly, attaching them to leaves and water-weeds. Some species wrap each egg carefully in a leaf for protection.

ABLED FROGS
esop wrote of the are's unhappiness t being prey to so nany animals. But hen it saw the frog's light, it felt more fortunate.

RED FOR DANGER!
Like the tiger salamander opposite, the mandarin newt has bright colors warning that it makes a foul mouthful. It lives in Asia.

FOAM NEST
he foam-nest tree rog whips up a ubbly nest to keep he spawn moist. When grown, tadpoles rop out into the pond eneath.

MATING
Early spring is a time of commotion in the pond as amphibians gather to breed. The male common frog struggles with rivals to find a female, and then takes up a piggyback position. He may stay there for many days, clasping her slippery chest skin tightly with roughened pads on his thumbs. As the eggs are laid, he sheds sperm over them. The exhausted pair then part company.

MALE MIDWIFE
The midwife toad is in fact the "husband," who gathers the egg string and carries it around his back legs for up to a month. As the tadpoles begin to hatch he releases them into a pool.

This 18th-century engraving is an impression of how a male midwife toad carries its eggs

Hunters in the water

MORE THAN 300 MILLION YEARS AGO, the reptiles appeared on Earth. They probably evolved from amphibians (pp. 38-39). Their big advantage was that they had made a complete break from life in water. Unlike amphibians, which needed water in which to lay their jelly-covered eggs, reptiles had hard-shelled eggs that could be laid on land. Soon, as dinosaurs, they would come to dominate life on land. Since that time, however, some groups of reptiles have made an "evolutionary U-turn" and gone back to life in the water. Many snakes readily take to water, swim well, and hunt fish, frogs, aquatic insects, and land creatures that come to the pond or riverbank for a drink. Indeed, certain groups of reptiles, such as crocodiles and turtles, have never really left their watery environment, though they come on to land to lay their eggs.

GIANT IN THE WATER
One of the longest, and certainly the heaviest, of snakes is the water boa, or anaconda, of northern South America. Lengths of 30 ft (9 m) and weights of over 440 lb (200 kg) have been recorded. It can consume creatures as large as a pig.

Water moccasin

DOWN IN THE SWAMPS
This old engraving shows the water moccasin, a venomous swamp dweller of the southeastern U.S. When this snake is threatened it opens its mouth wide to reveal the white inside lining, hence its other name of "cottonmouth."

Viperine water snake

Zig zag markings on the snake's back are similar to those of a common viper, or adder

Snake swims by wave-like motions of its body

Turtle…or terrapin?

There is little biological difference between a turtle and a terrapin. Most experts call the entire group (chelonians) turtles. Small freshwater species may be named terrapins, from a North American Indian word that referred originally to the diamondback terrapin. But the numerous exceptions confuse the issue. Whatever our labels, however, many turtles are well equipped for an aquatic life, either in fresh water or in the sea. Some have webbed or flipperlike feet and leathery skin covering the shell on their underside, through which oxygen can be absorbed. They tend to eat anything, from aquatic animals to the fruit of bankside trees to the remains of dead creatures.

CARCELY A RIPPLE
he viperine water snake of Europe is quite at home
the water, swimming easily across its surface.
will strike at just about any suitably sized prey,
om fish to frogs and even small mammals.
dults grow to 2.5 ft (80 cm) or more
his one is about life-sized,
ut young). Despite its name and
s zig zag markings like the
dder's, it is a
lative of the
rass snake and
not poisonous.

Yellow-bellied
terrapin

*Distinctive brown
and yellow markings*

OPPOSITE FEET FORWARD
The yellow-bellied terrapin may walk along the bed of a river or lake, or swim by paddling alternately with two limbs - the front foot on one side and the back foot on the other.

*Left-hand foreleg is
forward when right-hand
foreleg is back*

*Smooth plates
on shell*

*Shell lacks
bony plates*

*Ridged bony plates
on shell*

*Strong horny
jaws in mouth*

Soft-shelled turtle

*Webbed feet
for swimming*

THE SOFT SHELL
Soft-shelled turtles lack the hard, bony plates carried by the hard-shelled types. This life-size youngster will grow to about 1 ft (30 cm) long.

SNAPPY CUSTOMER
This young common snapper will reach almost 20 in (50 cm) when adult. Its strong, sharp-ridged jaws will be able to crack the shells of other turtles, which form part of its diet.

Common snapper

Vater snakes will eat all kinds of freshwater life,
ncluding this unfortunate frog

DIVING DRAGON
Eastern water dragons live in watercourses in eastern Australia. This lizard is a powerful swimmer, using its vertically flattened tail and long legs. It has a body length of nearly 3 ft (1 m), a tail more than double this, and it eats all kinds of water and shore life, from worms and frogs to shellfish, small mammals, and fruit.

Eastern water dragon

41

Floating flowers

IN ANCIENT TIMES people were amazed to see that, when a previously dry watercourse filled with recent rains, the splendid blooms of water lilies would soon appear.

Flower b

These aquatic plants gained a reputation as a symbol of immortality; the ancient Egyptians even worshipped one type of water lily, the sacred lotus. Water lily flowers are made more mysterious by their daily routine: they remain closed during the morning, open to reveal their beauty at around noon, and towards evening close again and sink slightly into the water. This may be an adaptation to aid pollination by flying insects, which are more likely to be active in the afternoon's warmth. On overcast days they might not open fully at all. During gray weather, signaling wind and rain, the closed flowers are less likely to be swamped. The flowers and leaves grow on tough, rubbery stems - 10 ft (3 m) long in some species - anchored in the mud on the beds of ponds, lakes, and slow rivers.

THE "BEAUTIFUL NUISANCE"
The water hyacinth is a free-floating flowering plant that spreads rapidly, often clogging rivers, canals, and ditches.

Red hybrid - "Escarboucle

Leaves may be heart shaped, oval, or round

Yellow water lily leaves are patterned with a red tinge

White water lily flower

Leathery leaves repel water droplets

Pink hybrid

Noticeable yellow stamens

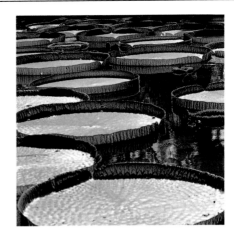

LILIES AND THEIR HYBRIDS
There are some 60 species of water lily around
the world (in some areas they are known as lotuses).
Their beautiful waxy-looking flowers and bold
circular leaves have made them favorites in ponds,
ornamental water gardens, and landscaped lakes.
Plant growers have bred many differently
colored flowers.

Yellow hybrid -
"Chromatella"

Waxy petals

Pink hybrid

FLOATING SAUCERS
Some of the largest leaves of any plant
belong to the Amazonian water lily.
A single leaf may be more than 5 ft (1.5 m)
across, with an upturned rim and stiff
reinforcing ribs beneath.

LILY LEAF CASE
The china mark moth's caterpillar cuts out
an oval of leaf and fastens it to the underside
with silk thread
to form a
protective
case.

Water lily
leaf

WELL-USED LEAVES
The leaves (lily "pads") are used by many water creatures.
Pond snails browse on them and lay their speckled, jelly-sausage
egg masses (p. 8) on their undersides. Frogs rest on or under them,
waiting to snap up unwary insects. In some places the pads grow so
densely that certain creatures can walk on them. The African jaçana
bird has long, widespread toes and is known as the "lily trotter,"
as it steps delicately on the leaves in search of insects and seeds.

Plants at the pond's surface

MANY WATER PLANTS are not rooted in the mud at the bottom of the pond but are free to float over the surface of the water. Most have trailing roots that balance the plant and absorb minerals, and some have no roots at all. At first sight, these plants seem to have few problems. Unlike some land plants, they are well supported and, out in the middle of the pond, they cannot be shaded by trees or taller plants. But there are disadvantages: the water's surface can be whipped by the wind into waves that drag and tear at them, rain might collect on a leaf and sink it, or the leaf may be frozen under water!

SMALLEST PLANTS
The duckweeds are among the smallest and simplest flowering plants in the world. Flowers are produced only in shallow water that receives plenty of sunlight. The "leaves" contain air-filled spaces called lacunae that keep them afloat.

Tiny roots absorb minerals from the water

Blanket weed

Surface view

Side view

Duckweed

Three of the many species of duckweed are shown here

Pale-green mass is made up of hundreds of threadlike plants

New plants produced by side shoots that break off and float away

A GREEN BLANKET
"Blanket weed" is a popular name for the green hairlike masses of algae that burst into growth in the spring. These plants can spread so quickly that they cover the surface like a blanket of green wool, blocking out light to the plants below.

Two new leaves developing from old leaf

Ivy-leaved duckweed

Water lily leaf and flower bud (pp. 42-43)

FLOWERING FLOATER
This engraving shows another species of duckweed that floats on the water surface only when it is flowering; otherwise it floats just under the water surface. The ivy-leaf shape is formed when two new leaves develop, one on each side of the original leaf.

CIRCLE OF STRENGTH
Like many other floating leaves, those of water lilies have a rounded outline. This design probably helps to prevent tearing, when wind ruffles the pond surface. The shiny upper surface repels rainwater so that the leaves are not swamped by a shower. Lilies are not true floating plants because they are rooted in the mud (pp. 42-43).

Azolla water fern

Pink tinge develops to deep red in autumn

Threadlike roots trail beneath the plant

Leaves are similar in shape to water lily leaves

WINTER SEEDS AND BUDS

Frogbit, a relative of water soldier (below), has a similar way of avoiding the ice and frost of winter. In this case, however, the parts that survive the winter are the seeds and the specially grown, dense "winter buds." Both are produced in the autumn and sink to rest in the mud, until the increasing light levels and temperatures of spring spur them into growth, when they float to the surface again. In summer, the delicate white flowers and kidney-shaped leaves carpet whole ponds and ditches.

FLOATING FRONDS

Azolla is not a flowering plant but a fern, so technically its delicately sculptured "leaves" are called fronds. Tiny hairs repel water and keep the fronds from becoming waterlogged and sinking.

Frogbit

Plants will sometimes root in shallow water

Trailing roots

Water soldier

GREEN ROSETTES

The rosettes of water soldier spend summer floating at or near the pond surface. As autumn approaches, the leaves develop a limy coating that weighs them down. The plant sinks, avoiding winter's frost and ice. Fresh spring leaves lift it up again. This plant reproduces by sending out runners that root at a distance, and by male and female flowers borne on separate plants.

WATER SOLDIER IN FLOWER

White flowers are produced in midsummer, with male and female flowers on different plants. Once flowering is over, the plant sinks to the bottom of the pond.

Long, unbranched roots hang down under the plant to balance it

Underwater weeds

Submerged weeds grow in ponds and rivers like trees in a miniature underwater forest. They provide shelter for some animals, and places of ambush for others which dash and grab unwary victims swimming by. The weeds are food for many creatures, from pond snails to ducks. They also provide that most vital substance, oxygen. As a plant carries out photosynthesis, capturing the sun's light energy to build new tissues, it produces oxygen as a by-product. The oxygen filters into the water and is used by both plants and animals for the process of respiration. On a sunny day, small bubbles of oxygen can be seen coating underwater plants and occasionally rising to the surface.

Rigid hornwort

CURTAIN OF ROOTS
The water violet's abundant roots hang like a veil in the water. The stem grows out of the water, where it bears not leaves but pale, pinkish five-petaled flowers.

Water violet

TOTAL SUBMERSION
Feathery-looking hornworts are completely at home in the water. Even the flowers are submerged, growing where the leaf joins the stem.

New Zealand pygmyweed

GREEN BALL
Volvox is a microscopic water plant and an important food for tiny creatures.

Trailing roots

Canadian waterweed

NEW ZEALAND PYGMYWEED
This plant is causing concern in many waterways because of its uncontrolled spread. It was first introduced to bring oxygen into the water.

ACROSS THE ATLANTIC
Canadian waterweed left its North American home in about 1840, soon colonizing and clogging up European ponds and rivers.

POND "PLANKTON"
At 25X magnification, the microscopic world of underwater plants is revealed.

PERCH IN THE GRASS
Tape grass is one of the popularly named "river" grasses. It offers a hideout for fish, particularly the perch, which is camouflaged by its vertical stripes (p. 23).

Tape grass

Bulbous rush

Narrow leaves resemble the needles of a fir tree

SLENDER WATERWEED
The pale-green water starwort sways in clumps in the water.

FLUSHED RUSH
The bulbous rush is usually rooted on the pond's side, but sometimes it grows underwater, and becomes very long.

Water starwort

47

Dragonflies and damselflies

THESE LARGE, POWERFUL FLYERS speed back and forth along the bank and over the water's surface, using their enormous eyes to search out small creatures. Like those of other insects, the dragonfly's eyes are made up of many separate lenses that probably give a mosaic-like picture of the world. As the adults dart about above, the water-dwelling nymphs (babies) crawl on the pond bottom. Like their parents, they seize and eat any small creature they can catch, from other water insects to tadpoles and fish.

Cast-off nymphal skin

Broad-bodied libellula nymph   Young southern hawker nymph

Mask   Hooks on mask spear prey   Mask

THE DEADLY MASK
Dragonfly nymphs are the scourge of the pond, eating anything they can catch with their "mask." This is a horny flap, like the lower lip, which has two vicious hooks at the end (above). Normally the mask is folded under the head, but it is hinged so that it can suddenly shoot out to spear prey, which is then pulled back to the mouth.

Damselflies

These are smaller and more slender relatives of dragonflies. Although at first glance they appear very similar in shape and way of life, there are several important differences that set them apart from the dragonflies - most obviously the fact that the damselfly holds its two pairs of wings together over its back when resting, while the dragonfly holds them out flat at the sides of its body.

CAST-OFF CLOTHING
This perfectly detailed empty skin is from a brown hawker dragonfly's final molt. New adults usually emerge at night or early in the morning, to avoid enemies.

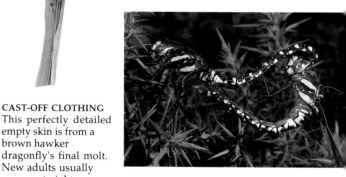

THE MATING GAME
The male dragonfly clasps the female and she bends to pick up the sperm from a special organ at the front of his abdomen.

SIMILAR WINGS
A damselfly's wings are roughly equal in size, with rounded ends, unlike the dragonfly's wings.

Blue-tailed damselfly

Emerald damselfly

MALE AND FEMALE
In most damselflies, the female has a slightly wider and less colorful abdomen than the male.

Eyes protrude from side of head

Rounded wing tips

Azure damselfly

Large red damselfly

SMALLER EYES
The small eyes of the damselfly are set on the sides of the head; the dragonfly's eyes meet at the top of the head.

WEAK FLYERS
Damselflies tend to be weaker flyers than their dragonfly cousins.

THE LIFE OF THE DRAGONFLY
A dragonfly begins life as an egg laid in water. It hatches into a larva that grows by splitting its skin and forming a new, larger skin. There are between eight and 15 molts over two years or more, depending on the species. A gradual change to adult form like this (compared with a sudden change; for example, caterpillar to butterfly) is called "incomplete metamorphosis." During the in-between stages the insect is referred to a nymph. Finally the nymph climbs up a stem into the air, splits its skin a final time, and the adult emerges.

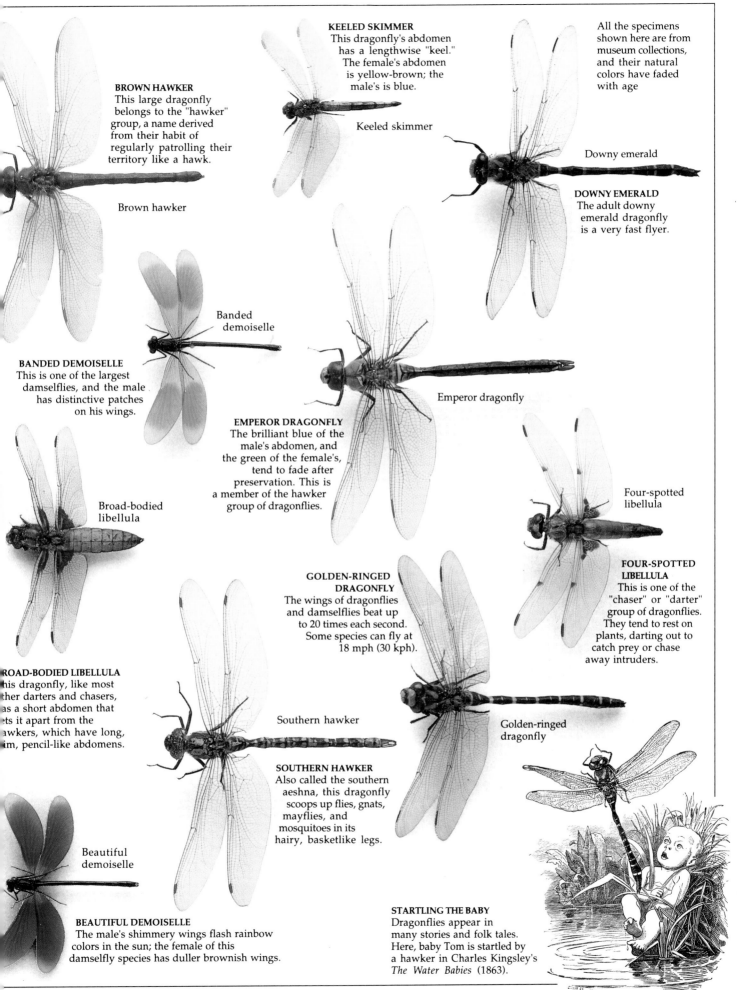

BROWN HAWKER
This large dragonfly belongs to the "hawker" group, a name derived from their habit of regularly patrolling their territory like a hawk.

Brown hawker

KEELED SKIMMER
This dragonfly's abdomen has a lengthwise "keel." The female's abdomen is yellow-brown; the male's is blue.

Keeled skimmer

All the specimens shown here are from museum collections, and their natural colors have faded with age

Downy emerald

DOWNY EMERALD
The adult downy emerald dragonfly is a very fast flyer.

Banded demoiselle

BANDED DEMOISELLE
This is one of the largest damselflies, and the male has distinctive patches on his wings.

Emperor dragonfly

EMPEROR DRAGONFLY
The brilliant blue of the male's abdomen, and the green of the female's, tend to fade after preservation. This is a member of the hawker group of dragonflies.

Broad-bodied libellula

BROAD-BODIED LIBELLULA
This dragonfly, like most other darters and chasers, has a short abdomen that sets it apart from the hawkers, which have long, slim, pencil-like abdomens.

Four-spotted libellula

FOUR-SPOTTED LIBELLULA
This is one of the "chaser" or "darter" group of dragonflies. They tend to rest on plants, darting out to catch prey or chase away intruders.

GOLDEN-RINGED DRAGONFLY
The wings of dragonflies and damselflies beat up to 20 times each second. Some species can fly at 18 mph (30 kph).

Southern hawker

SOUTHERN HAWKER
Also called the southern aeshna, this dragonfly scoops up flies, gnats, mayflies, and mosquitoes in its hairy, basketlike legs.

Golden-ringed dragonfly

Beautiful demoiselle

BEAUTIFUL DEMOISELLE
The male's shimmery wings flash rainbow colors in the sun; the female of this damselfly species has duller brownish wings.

STARTLING THE BABY
Dragonflies appear in many stories and folk tales. Here, baby Tom is startled by a hawker in Charles Kingsley's *The Water Babies* (1863).

49

Insects in the water

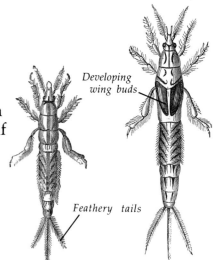

Developing wing buds

Insects, the most adaptable creatures on earth, can live in places ranging from glaciers to hot springs, from deserts to tropical forests. About half of the 25 major groups of insects live in fresh water. Some, such as water beetles and bugs, spend nearly all their lives in water. Others, like mayflies and caddis flies, have a watery "childhood" and emerge into the air when adult. Certain aquatic insects, including the water beetles, are air-breathing and visit the surface regularly to obtain supplies, which they store by various clever means (p. 51). Others have specialized "gills" to take oxygen from the water, and still others can absorb dissolved oxygen through their skin.

Feathery tails

Like dragonfly larvae (p. 48), mayfly larvae are called nymphs

As the nymph matur small "wing buds" grow with each mol

Rat-tailed maggots (drone fly larvae)

Adult drone fly

Adult mayfly

MAGGOT'S PARENT
The rat-tailed maggot is the larva of the drone fly, a type of hover fly, named because it looks like the drones of the honey bee.

Long "tails" identify this insect

Breathing tube

MAGGOT WITH SNORKEL *above*
The rat-tailed maggot has a long breathing tube of three sections that telescope into one another. It lives in the mud of shallow ponds, sucking up decaying food.

THREE-TAILED FLY
Like its larvae, the adult mayfly has three very distinctive trailing "tails." Mayflies are known as "spinners" by people who fish.

GROWN-UP CADDIS
Adult caddis flies are less well-known than their water-dwelling youngsters. The adults are drab gray or brown, come out at dusk or night, and are easily confused with small moths. They flit about near water, rarely feed, and seldom live more than a few days.

SPRING FEAST
Mayfly adults emerge in huge swarms in spring. They fly weakly, have no mouths and so cannot feed, and spend their few days of adult life mating and layin eggs by dipping their abdomens in water. The "dance of the mayflies" attracts hungry fish - and anglers (people who fish) who use mayfly lures to catch trout.

Adult caddis flies

Wings covered with fine hairs

Antennae often long as the body

STICKS AND STONES
Many species of caddis fly have aquatic larvae that build protective cases around themselves. The construction material is characteristic of each species. As the larva grows, it adds more material to the front of the case.

Larval cases may be attached to water plants or lie on the pond bottom

Small stones

Plant stalks

Discarded sn shells

Entrance to case

Case is extended by adding material to the front end

Head of larva emerges from case to feed

Every species makes a distinctive case

Cases built by caddisfly larvae

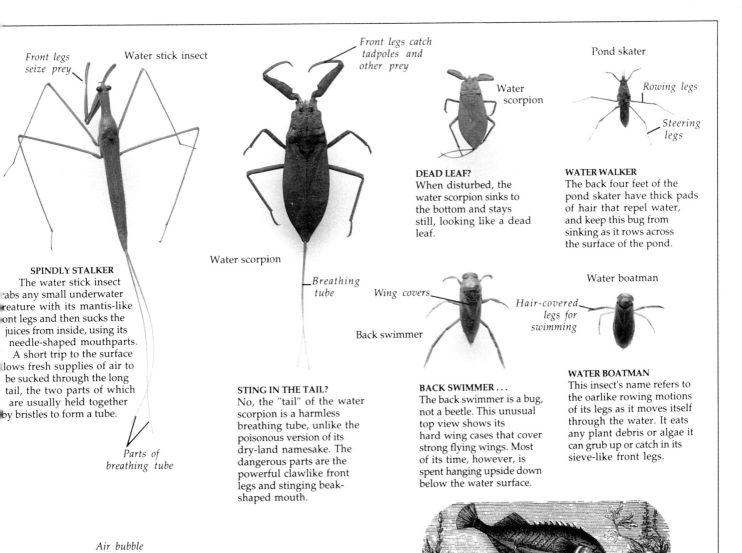

Front legs seize prey — Water stick insect

Front legs catch tadpoles and other prey

Water scorpion

Pond skater

Rowing legs

Steering legs

Water scorpion

DEAD LEAF?
When disturbed, the water scorpion sinks to the bottom and stays still, looking like a dead leaf.

WATER WALKER
The back four feet of the pond skater have thick pads of hair that repel water, and keep this bug from sinking as it rows across the surface of the pond.

SPINDLY STALKER
The water stick insect grabs any small underwater creature with its mantis-like front legs and then sucks the juices from inside, using its needle-shaped mouthparts. A short trip to the surface allows fresh supplies of air to be sucked through the long tail, the two parts of which are usually held together by bristles to form a tube.

Parts of breathing tube

Breathing tube

Wing covers

Back swimmer

Water boatman

Hair-covered legs for swimming

STING IN THE TAIL?
No, the "tail" of the water scorpion is a harmless breathing tube, unlike the poisonous version of its dry-land namesake. The dangerous parts are the powerful clawlike front legs and stinging beak-shaped mouth.

BACK SWIMMER . . .
The back swimmer is a bug, not a beetle. This unusual top view shows its hard wing cases that cover strong flying wings. Most of its time, however, is spent hanging upside down below the water surface.

WATER BOATMAN
This insect's name refers to the oarlike rowing motions of its legs as it moves itself through the water. It eats any plant debris or algae it can grub up or catch in its sieve-like front legs.

Air bubble

THE BUBBLE CHAMBER
The air-breathing water spider (not actually an insect but an arachnid) makes a "diving bell" to live in. It weaves a web among water plants and stocks it with air from the surface (below). The air being transported in its body hairs gives the spider's abdomen a silvery sheen (left).

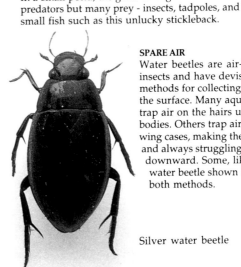

BEETLE POWER
In a small pond, the great diving beetle has few predators but many prey - insects, tadpoles, and small fish such as this unlucky stickleback.

SPARE AIR
Water beetles are air-breathing insects and have devised clever methods for collecting air from the surface. Many aquatic beetles trap air on the hairs under their bodies. Others trap air under their wing cases, making them buoyant and always struggling to swim downward. Some, like the silver water beetle shown here, use both methods.

Silver water beetle

Freshwater shells

ALL THE LIFE-SIZED SHELLS shown here have two features in common: their builder-owners live in fresh water, and they belong to the mollusk group. The mollusk's shell is made chiefly of calcium-containing minerals such as calcium carbonate (lime). To make its shell, the animal must absorb minerals from the water. In general, aquatic mollusks are more common in "hard-water" areas, where water is naturally richer in dissolved minerals. The mussels and cockles (bivalves) feed by sucking in a stream of water and filtering out tiny food particles. Most snails and limpets (gastropods) "graze", on water plants and the algal "scum" on submerged stones, but some species can filter-feed.

SEVEN SEASONS
The growth rings on this swan mussel's shell show that it is about six or seven years old.

How do mollusks breathe?

Water snails are divided into two groups, depending on how they breathe. The great pond snail, ram's-horn snail, and bladder snail are known as pulmonates - they breathe air, like land snails. They float up to the surface, open a breathing aperture (hole) and take a gulp of air into a lung-like cavity. The other group, including valve, river, and spire snails, are called prosobranchs. They breathe by absorbing oxygen from the water through gills.

DUCK MUSSEL
This bivalve's shell is more swollen than that of the swan mussel.

RIGHT-HANDERS
Usually great pond snail shells curl to the right, but "left-handers" are known.

SEE-THROUGH SNAIL
The nautilus ram's-horn is so small that its shell is semi-transparent.

BIVALVE LARDER
Pea mussels are the staple food of many fish and water birds.

WANDERING SNAIL
The whorls of this wandering snail are squashed up at its tip.

CURLY WHORLY
The tightly coiled white ram's-horn is from ponds and streams.

MARBLED SNAIL
The nerite snail has an attractively speckled and whorled shell.

JOINTED SHELL
The horny pea cockle is a bivalve mollusk as it has two shells.

River shellfish

The mollusks below and left (swan and duck mussels) tend to live in flowing water, rather than the still waters of ponds and lakes. The growth rings of the mussels indicate their age, which might be up to a dozen years for a large individual. Growth rings can be seen on snails, too, but they are less clearly divided into a year-by-year pattern.

Snails grow by adding new material at the open end of the shell

TWISTING TUBE
Snail shells are coiled, gradually widening tubes, clearly seen on this Lister's river snail.

MINERAL COLLECTOR
River snail's shells may be over 2 in (5 cm) long - a lot of calcium to collect.

LISTENING SNAIL
The ear pond snail's flared opening resembles a human ear.

SWOLLEN JOINT
This tumid unio mussel has an inflated "umbo" near its hinge line.

ZEBRA MUSSEL
This bivalve is anchored to rocks by sticky threads.

WATERWEED EATER
The great ram's-horn water snail browses on underwater plants.

DISTINCTIVE SHELL
The last whorl on the bladder snail's shell is very large.

STUBBY AND SHINY
These shiny, compact shells belong to the common bithynia.

BITHYNIA LEACHI
These bithynias have no common name; only a scientific name.

STRAIGHT SNAIL
The river limpet is a true snail, but its shell is not coiled.

OPEN AND SHUT
The "valve" of the valve snail is the door or operculum, of its shell.

SLOW WATER
The lake limpet can often be found in slow-flowing rivers.

OPENING THE DOOR
The operculum, or door, to the shell allows the snail to emerge to feed.

Operculum makes a watertight seal to shell when closed

TWO TINY SHELLS
Pea shell cockles are tiny, filter-feeding bivalve mollusks.

SALTY AND FRESH
Jenkin's spire shells are found in estuaries as well as in ponds and rivers.

The head of the river

MANY RIVERS begin life as fast-flowing upland streams, cascading across open areas or through craggy woodlands. The deep, rocky gulleys, the overhanging trees, and the splashing waters create contrasting worlds: damp, shady banks with lush green vegetation, and stream beds where rushing water washes away nearly all plant life and any but the most stubbornly clinging animals. In a flood, entire plant and animal communities may be swept away. Yet somehow new seeds and spores soon spring up, and creatures creep out from under rocks to fight their way back upstream.

Dipper

UNDERWATER WALKER
The dipper bobs its head as it stands on midstream rocks, watching for small animal prey. It can also walk along the river-bed, head facing upstream and tail acting as a rudder in the current, to keep its feet firmly on the bottom.

ARMORED CRAYFISH
Hard (mineral-rich) water is favored by the freshwater crayfish, a relative of the marine lobster. It needs plenty of calcium minerals to build its shell.

Hard outer shell made up from minerals in the water

Freshwater crayfish

BANKSIDE MOISTURE LOVERS
Succulent growths of mosses, liverworts, ferns, and other damp-loving plants colonize the banks and splash-zone rocks. The larger heart-shaped leaves are marsh violet.

Polytrichum moss

Fern

Puffball

Liverwort

YOUNG BALL
Fungi, such as this young member of the puffball group, prefer shady stream-side conditions.

LICHEN BRANCH
Shady, damp conditions are ideal for certain lichens, which are co-operative combinations of fungi and algae. Two different kinds of leafy lichen are growing on this branch.

Marsh violet

Great wood rush

Liverwort

Bullhead

UPSTREAM FISH
Despite the fast current fish, such as the bullhead, are found at the head of the river. The bullhead's flattened shape allows it to hide under stones.

Oak leaves

FOOD FROM ABOVE
Trees such as the oak hang
over the water, and if their
fruits and leaves fall into the
water they provide food for
river-dwellers.

Fontinalis
moss

Acorns

*Galls (swellings) caused
by insects*

*Deeply divided
fronds*

Great wood rush

BETWEEN THE BOULDERS
Groups of midstream boulders
often support a thriving
island of life; here, great
wood rush sprouts from soil
collected by the current.

UNDERWATER MOSS
Fontinalis or "willow moss," anchored to a
stone or fallen log, moves back and forth with
the current in slower streams and rivers.

*Shiny,
undivided
fronds*

*Rows of
spores*

*Layer of moss
growing on
boulders*

Male fern

FEATHERY FRONDS
Many types of ferns thrive in the
shaded, humid conditions along
riverbanks. The hart's-tongue
fern (far right) has riblike
rows of brown spore cases
on the undersides of its fronds.
It is unusual among ferns
in having solid,
unbranched fronds.

*Feathery,
pale-green
fronds*

*Shiny,
dark-green
fronds*

Hard-
fern

Lady fern

Hart's-tongue
fern

Brown spore cases

55

Life along the riverbank

As STREAMS BECOME MORE SEDATE and their courses join up and widen, the river comes into being. But when does a stream become a river? One definition is that streams are less than 15 ft (5 m) wide, while rivers are more. Larger rivers usually have a slower current, allowing rooted plants to grow well at the water's edge. Whatever the distinction, riverbank life suits many kinds of plants and animals. On a high-banked river, the soil at the water's edge is nearly always saturated, but it becomes drier higher up the bank. So plant life often grows in zones, with mud-rooted irises and water plantains lower down, and the damp-ground hemp agrimony, balsam, and similar flowers slightly higher.

Thistle-shaped flower head

Hooks attach fruits to passing animals

ABOUT TO FLOWER
This teasel's flower is just coming out, its pinkish-mauve petals not yet visible.

FIVE IN ONE
Each small "flower" of hemp agrimony is a cluster of five even smaller "florets."

Teasel

Spiny flower head is still developing

Heart-shaped leaves are slightly downy

Exploring along the river has long been a favorite leisure pastime

Explosive seedcases are developing inside the flowers

Hemp agrimony

HITCHING A RIDE
Young great burdock flowers already bear the hooks that, when the seeds ripen, will catch on fur, coats, and socks.

Leaves have toothed edges

TRAVELING FLOWER
Indian, or Himalayan, balsam, a native of that region, has spread along many riverbanks, ditch sides and damp gulleys.

Leaves have serrated margins

Stem has reddish tinge

Indian balsam
(Himalayan balsam)

HIGH-WATER MARK
The river's spring flood left surface debris stuck to this overhanging twig, 3 ft (1 m) above summer's water level.

Old plant stalks caught around twig

The pyramid-shaped blossoms make water plantain a dramatic plant on the riverbank.

Water plantain leaf

RIVERBANK HOME
Many mammals use the riverbank as a home. Otters live in well-hidden "holts" in the bank vegetation or under overhanging tree roots.

DOWN IN THE MUD
The beds of ponds and rivers abound with small animals such as these, which are food for fish and other creatures.

Flatworm

Freshwater shrimp

The caddis larva has built its case from tiny pebbles (p. 50)

Flatworm

Freshwater shrimp

Toothmarks of mammal

Loaches

BARBEL-BEARD
The barbels, or "whiskers," of the loach are used as feeling organs. This river dweller emerges from under stones after dusk to hunt in the mud for worms, insects, and other small water life.

Water starwort provides cover for these shy fish

Water plantain blossoms

AFTERNOON OPENING
Water plantain roots in the mud at the edges of small rivers. Its flowers are closed for most of the morning and evening, and open only after noon.

Tiny lilac flowers

Yellow flag leaves

Tiny mollusks attached to stone

ANONYMOUS NIBBLER
These yellow flag leaves from a steep riverbank have been nibbled by a hungry mammal.

CLAMPING DOWN
Under their rounded shells, the "feet" of these tiny freshwater mollusks grasp this rock firmly.

The river's mouth

AT LAST the river's course is ended. Its banks curl outward to become the seashore, and the tide brings in salt water that begins to impose itself on the plant and animal life. The last stretch of a river is known as the estuary, and it is here that the river's currents slow down to a crawl and the smallest mud and silt particles slowly settle on the bed and banks. The water, mixed by waves and tides, is often cloudy so submerged plants are rare, since they do not receive enough light for photosynthesis (p. 10). Relatively few plants and animals are adapted to the enormous variations in salt concentration, but those that are face little competition and so are often found in huge numbers. The specimens shown below were all collected from an estuary, to give some idea of the range of animals and plants that can be found at the mouth of the river.

MOLTED FEATHERS
Discarded feathers are a common find on the estuary and are evidence of the species that live there.

Molted feathers

Washed-up bone

Gull

ESTUARY GULL
The rich animal life of the estuary attracts gulls of all kinds.

DISCARDED SKELETONS
Among the treasures you can find washed up on the edge of the estuary are various bones.

Glasswort

Sea spurge

GLASS FROM PLANTS
The glassworts are so named because in former times their ashes (being high in sodium carbonate) were used to make glass. They are common on estuaries and salt marshes (p. 60) and have thick, juicy leaves.

Fleshy leaves store water

CREEPING ABOUT
The sea spurge's creeping stem spreads through the sand dunes at the river's mouth. Like glasswort, it has thick, fleshy leaves.

DINNERTIME AT LOW TIDE
Flocks of oystercatchers and other waders crow[d] on to the estuary mud at low tide, pecking and probing for worms, shrimps, shellfish, and crab[s]

Glasswort

Sea sandwort

Eel grass

Feather[s]

Roots begin to stabilize estuary mud

ESTUARY DUMP
The calmer waters of the estuary's tidal inlets are nature's dumping ground for all kinds of seaside debris, from dried-out seaweeds and ee[l] grass to feathers, bits of weeds, and dead crabs.

ystercatcher chicks hatch from eggs laid in open or short
getation around the estuary. The chicks can take
to 26 weeks to learn the specialized
eding techniques from their
rents.

Winkles

Tellina

Cockle

Periwinkle

Mussel

Young crab

Oyster shell

Tellina shell

Cockleshell

HOLE IN ONE
These mollusk shells
have been pecked through
by estuary birds and the animal
inside has been eaten.

Oystercatcher
and chick

UNDER THE BREAKWATER
Any "obstruction" on the
flat estuary, such as a
breakwater or pier, soon
becomes colonized by a
variety of life that can
tolerate the different salt
levels. The sea slater is a crustacean,
cousin of the wood louse, and also
a relative of the crab.

Sea slater

*Hole pecked
by bird*

ockleshell

Tellina shell

Lugworm

Oyster
shell

SHORE WORM
Squiggly marks on
the estuary mud
mark the position of a
lugworm's U-shaped burrow.

Slipper
limpet

Cockle-
shell

Sheldrake
and chick

Barnacles

Razor shell

IN FROM THE SEA
The shells of true seashore
mollusks are often washed
up on the estuary shore,
as was this small barnacle-
encrusted stone, loosened
by a storm.

SHELDRAKE DUCKLING
Young sheldrakes look like most other
ducklings, but the adults look more like
geese. This waterfowl eats not only
shellfish but also fish, worms, and other
small animals.

Crab

PIPEFISH
This relative
of the seahorse has
hardened outer skin
and moves using
its dorsal (back) fin.
It copes well in the
changing salt levels
of estuary water.

Pipefish

Spiral wrack

SHORE WEED
In the more sheltered and
seaward sites, shore algae can gain
a foothold. This spiral wrack is characteristic
of the upper shore zone.

The salt marsh

MANY ESTUARIES (p. 58) are flanked by a broad expanse of land, riddled with creeks and channels, and the salty soil supports its own very distinctive plant population. This is the salt marsh and it is a very forbidding habitat for plants. Twice each day, sea water pours through the drainage channels and its salt soaks into the soil and mud. As the tide retreats, evaporation leaves behind a salty residue. Spring tides flood the entire marsh with sea water. Yet a few hours later, at low tide, heavy rain may have turned the surface into an almost freshwater habitat. The plants growing on a salt marsh have become specially adapted to such changing conditions.

PINKS AND PURPLES
Many salt-marsh plants have pink, lavender, or purple flowers, coloring the whole marsh when in bloom. They tend to flower later in summer or in the autumn.

Flower head

MARSH GRASS
The flower heads of couch grass show in this clump of grasses from the higher, drier part of the marsh.

Sea aster

Flowerspike

PLAIN PLANTAIN
The unremarkable-looking sea plantain populates the flat areas of the salt marsh.

Sea plantain

PURPLE AND YELLOW
In late summer and early autumn, the distinctive flowers of sea aster carpet large areas of salt marsh.

Flower stalk arises from clump of fleshy leaves

SEA LAVENDER
In late summer the flowers of the sea lavender turn the salt marsh lilac.

Flower-spike

Couch grass

Leaves have a bluish tinge

SEA ARROW GRASS
Look among the grassy stems of the marsh and you will find the juicy stems of sea arrow grass. Despite its name, it is not a true grass.

Sea lavender

Sea arrow grass

SILVER-GREEN LEAVES
The silvery leaves are covered with tiny air-filled protective scales. Sea purslane grows along the edges of the channels and creeks within the salt marsh.

Ripening seed heads

Sea purslane

Leaves take up or lose water as the salt level changes

FLESHY LEAVES
The thick, fleshy leaves of salt-marsh dwellers are well represented by this annual seablite.

Juicy leaves store water

BINDING IN THE MARSH
Cord grass, an early colonizer of the bare mud, is often planted on the lower parts of marshes and estuaries to stabilize them with its underground stems and thick root system.

Cord grass

RICH PICKINGS
Knots and other wading birds probe the mud of salt-marsh channels for food.

Glasswort

Swollen, jointed stems store water

Annual seablite

The leaves produce salt crystals to rid the plant of excess salt

Thick roots

SALT-MARSH STABILIZER
Glasswort is one of the first plants to colonize the estuary mud, its delicate roots beginning the stabilizing process.

TIDAL DEBRIS
Each tide sweeps old stems, bits of crabs, and other debris along the channels that riddle the marsh.

Crabs

CAST-UP REMAINS
Young shore crabs, young cockles, and a whelk's spongy, empty egg case are some of the items found when "marsh-combing" along the channel edges.

SQUELCHING OOZE
This is the stuff of life in the salt marsh and estuary - thick, shiny mud, rich in organic matter.

Empty shells

Salt-marsh mud

Roots bind the slippery mud

Whelk egg case

Study and conservation

T HE FASCINATING WILDLIFE OF PONDS AND RIVERS is suffering in our modern world. Pollution, the demand for housing and farm land, and more people using the water for relaxation and recreation are all taking their toll. Conserving and preserving our natural freshwater habitats is increasingly important. It begins with study and understanding. Students of nature are interested in what lives where, and why - and through observation rather than interference. When out on a field trip they have respect for nature, follow the country code, and obey the wildlife laws. If you wish to find out more about ponds and rivers, contact one of the organizations listed on page 64 for guidance on a voyage into nature's watery domain.

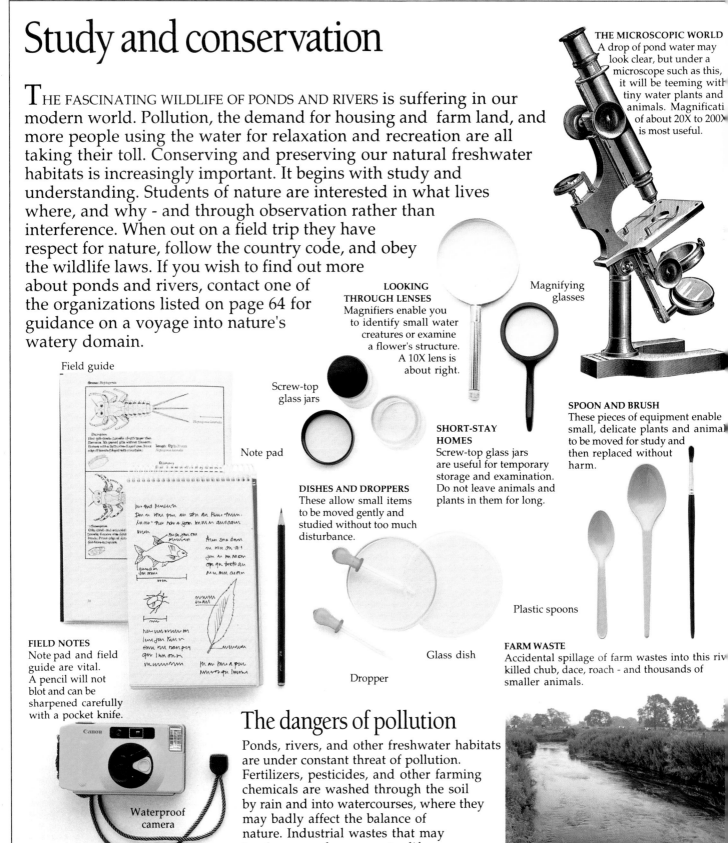

THE MICROSCOPIC WORLD
A drop of pond water may look clear, but under a microscope such as this, it will be teeming with tiny water plants and animals. Magnificati of about 20X to 200X is most useful.

Magnifying glasses

LOOKING THROUGH LENSES
Magnifiers enable you to identify small water creatures or examine a flower's structure. A 10X lens is about right.

Screw-top glass jars

Note pad

SPOON AND BRUSH
These pieces of equipment enable small, delicate plants and animal to be moved for study and then replaced without harm.

SHORT-STAY HOMES
Screw-top glass jars are useful for temporary storage and examination. Do not leave animals and plants in them for long.

DISHES AND DROPPERS
These allow small items to be moved gently and studied without too much disturbance.

Plastic spoons

Field guide

FIELD NOTES
Note pad and field guide are vital. A pencil will not blot and can be sharpened carefully with a pocket knife.

Glass dish

Dropper

FARM WASTE
Accidental spillage of farm wastes into this riv killed chub, dace, roach - and thousands of smaller animals.

The dangers of pollution

Ponds, rivers, and other freshwater habitats are under constant threat of pollution. Fertilizers, pesticides, and other farming chemicals are washed through the soil by rain and into watercourses, where they may badly affect the balance of nature. Industrial wastes that may enter rivers can damage water life for long stretches downstream. Most authorities have clean-water laws, but these are not always observed; "accidents" happen, and inspectors cannot monitor every backwater. We can all contribute, by reporting suspicions to the authorities, or by volunteering to help clean out and restock a weed-choked pond, or by clearing a stream used as a rubbish tip.

Waterproof camera

DAMP-PROOF SNAPS
Modern waterproof cameras allow photographs to be taken in the wettest places, even in the spray of a fast stream. Photos record nature without disturbing it.

Folding
pocket
knife

Plant cutter

Plastic bags
and ties

WATERPROOFING
Aquatic plants dry out
quickly in air. Keep them
wet by carrying them in
plastic bags.

Fine-mesh sieve

CLEAN CUT
Take plant samples only with permission,
and with a sharp blade for minimum damage.

Fork

Trowel

Sealable plastic containers

SPLASH-PROOF CONTAINERS
Pack animals carefully in
sealable containers, using
waterweed as "padding"
to minimize splashing.

SIEVE FOR SORTING
A fine-mesh sieve can
be rocked gently in
water to sort small
animals from mud
and silt.

TAKING A SAMPLE
A bucket on a string
can be tossed from a
bridge, bank, or boat
to sample the water.

SMALL DIGGERS
If you are permitted to dig up plants
or search for muddy-bottom
creatures, use a clean, sharp
fork or trowel and take
great care.

Water-sampling
bucket

Large-mesh net

Fine-mesh net

NET RESULTS
Nets have different mesh
(sizes) for large or small specimens.
Be careful not to uproot plants.
After sorting, replace the net's contents in the water
as quickly as possible.

Index

A

alder, 19, 20
annual seablites, 61
arrowheads, 14, 20
azolla, 45

B

back swimmers, 51
barnacles, 59
beavers, 37
birch, 19
bithynias, 53
bitterlings, 25
bitterns, 31
bittersweet, 21
blanket weeds, 44
bleak, 22
bream, 23
bullheads, 55

C

caddis flies, 19, 50, 57
carnivores, 10, 12
carp, 12, 13, 24, 25
china mark moths, 43
cockles, 52, 53, 59
common snappers, 41
cord grass, 61
cotton grass, 10
couch grass, 61
crabs, 58, 61

D

damselflies, 48, 49
dippers, 54

dragonflies, 12, 13, 17, 48, 49
drone flies, 50
ducks, 28, 29, 59
duckweeds, 6, 9, 13, 44

E

ecology, 12, 34
eel grass, 47, 58
eels, 22, 24

F

ferns, 54, 55
figwort, 10, 14, 18
flatworms, 13, 20, 57
fool's watercress, 34
freshwater crayfish, 54
freshwater shrimps, 57
frogs, 8, 9, 12, 20, 38, 39
fungi, 19, 54

G

glasswort, 58, 61
gnats, 16
grass carp, 25
great burdock, 56
greater spearwort, 15
greater willow herb, 14
great wood rush, 54, 55
grebes, 30, 31
gudgeon, 25
gulls, 58

H

hawthorn, 15
hemp agrimony, 14, 18, 56
herbivores, 10, 12, 17
herons, 12, 30, 31
hermaphrodites, 8

I

Indian balsam, 56
irises, 6, 7, 11, 15, 19, 21, 35, 56, 57

K

kingcups, 7
kingfishers, 30
Kingsley, Charles, 49
knots, 61

L

lady's-smock, 6
leeches, 9, 13
lichens, 54
limpets, 53, 59
liverworts, 54
loach, 57
loosestrife, 14
lugworms, 59

M

mare's-tails, 11, 12, 34
marsh marigolds, 7
mayflies, 9, 13, 17, 50-1
meadow rue, 7
meadowsweet, 14
metamorphosis, 12, 48
midges, 16
mink, 12, 36
mosquitoes, 16
mosses, 54, 55
mussels, 52, 53, 59

N

nerites, 52
newts, 8, 9, 12, 16, 19, 38-9
New Zealand pygmyweed, 46

O

oaks, 19, 55
otters, 37, 57
oysters, 59
oystercatchers, 58, 59

P

perch, 23
periwinkles, 59
photosynthesis, 10, 20, 46
pikes, 24
pintail ducks, 18, 29
pipefishes, 59
plankton, 47
pond skaters, 17, 20, 51
poplars, 7
puss moths, 7

R

ragged robin, 10
rat-tailed maggots, 50
razor shells, 59
reed buntings, 30, 31
reed grasses, 6
reed mace, 10, 19, 33, 34, 35
reeds, 6, 10, 21, 32-5
reed warblers, 30, 31
rigid hornwort, 46
roach, 23
rudd, 22
rushes, 14, 18, 32-5, 47

S

St.-John's-wort, 14-16
salmon, 23
sea arrow grass, 60
sea aster, 61
sea lavender, 61
sea plantain, 60
sea purslane, 61
sea spurge, 58
sedges, 6, 11, 18, 19, 32-5
slaters, 9, 12, 59
snails, 8, 12, 16, 19, 20, 52, 53
snakes, 40-41
snipe, 30, 31
spiral wrack, 59
sticklebacks, 9, 17, 25, 51
swans, 18, 28, 29

T

teal, 28
teasels, 56
tellinas, 59
tench, 12, 22
toads, 8, 12, 16, 20, 38-9
trout, 26-7
turtles, 41

V

violets, 46, 54
volvox, 46

W

water arum, 10, 14
water beetles, 9, 12, 13, 17, 50-1
water bistort, 14
water boatmen, 13, 16, 51
water crowfoot, 6, 9, 13
water fleas, 8
water forget-me-not, 15
water hawthorn, 17
water hyacinth, 42
water lilies, 8, 10, 20, 34, 42-3, 44
water mites, 13
water plantain, 7, 15, 56, 57
water rail, 31
water shrews, 12, 36
water scorpions, 51
water soldiers, 45
water spiders, 51
water starwort, 47, 57
water stick insects, 17, 51
waterweeds, 19, 47
whelks, 61
widgeon, 28
willows, 7, 11, 15, 19, 21, 34, 35
winkles, 59

Y

yellow flags, 7, 11, 15, 19, 21, 57

Useful addresses

American Fisheries Society
5410 Grosvenor Lane,
Suite 100,
Bethesda, MD 20814-2199

National Wetlands
Conservation Project
c/o Nature Conservancy
1800 North Kent Street,
Suite 800,
Arlington, VA 22209

Sierra Club
330 Pennsylvania
Avenue, S.E.
Washington, D.C. 20003

National Audubon Society
National Capital Office,
645 Pennsylvania
Avenue, S.E.
Washington, D.C.
20036-2266

National Wildlife
Federation
1400 16th Street, N.W.
Washington, D.C.
20036-2266

U.S. Fish and
Wildlife Service
Publication Unit,
1717 H Street, N.W.,
Room 148
Washington, D.C. 20240

Acknowledgments

Picture credits
t=top b=bottom m=middle l=left r=right

Heather Angel: 43tr; 45br; 53br
G.I. Bernard/Oxford Scientific Films: 51ml
B.Borrell/Frank Lane Picture Agency: 39m
Bridgeman Art Library: 34tr
British Museum/Natural History: 48tl
B.B.Casals/Frank Lane Picture Agency: 39t
John Clegg: 47tl
G.Dore/Bruce Coleman Ltd: 48mr; 60tr
Fotomas Index: 39ml
C.B. and D.W. Frith/Bruce Coleman Ltd: 41br
Tom and Pam Gardener/Frank Lane Picture Agency: 38br
D.T. Grewcock/Frank Lane Picture Agency: 62br

Mark Hamblin/Frank Lane Picture Agency: 39bm
David Hosking/Eric and David Hosking: 27m; 37ml
Mansell Collection: 13m, tr, ml; 35ml; 49br
L.C. Marigo/Bruce Coleman Ltd: 42bl
Mary Evans Picture Library: 22tl; 23tr; 30bl; 40tr
Dr Morley Reed/Science Photo Library: 39bl
Jany Sauvanet/Natural History Photographic Agency: 40ml
Richard Vaughan/Ardea: 58mr
Roger Wilmshurst/Frank Lane Picture Agency: 29t

Illustrations by Coral Mula: 34bl; 36ml, bl, br; 35tl; ml; 38ml, m; 39mt

Picture research by: Millie Trowbridge

Dorling Kindersley would like to thank:
The Booth Museum of Natural History, Brighton.
Ed Wade, and Respectible Reptiles, Hampton, for help with the amphibians and reptiles.
Richard Harrison and Robert Hughes, Upwey Trout Hatchery, for help with the trout eggs.
Jane Parker for the index.
Fred Ford and Mike Pilley of Radius Graphics, and Ray Owen for artwork.
Anne-Marie Bulat for her work on the initial stages of the book.
Carole Ash, Neville Graham and Martyn Foote for design assistance.
Kim Taylor for special photography on page 27.
Dave King for special photography on pages 2-5, 28-31, 36-7, 52-3 and 62-3.

The author would like to thank:
Don Bentley for loan of equipment;
Mike Birch of Mickfield Fish Centre; Max Bond and Tim Watts of Framlingham Fisheries;
CEL Trout Farm, Woodbridge;
Keith Chell and Chris Riley of Slapton Ley Field Centre; Wendy and David Edwards, Ellen and Chris Nall, Jacqui and Tony Storer for allowing their ponds to be sampled; David "Biggles" Gooderham and Jane Parker for help with collecting; Andrea Hanks and staff at Thornham Magna Field Centre; Alastair MacEwan for technical advice; Ashley Morsely for fish care; Richard Weaving of Dawlish Warren Nature Reserve; John Wortley, Andy Wood and colleagues at Anglian Water Authority.